D1093605

THE WELL-DRESSED HOME

WITHDRAWN

# THE WELL-DRESSED HOME

Fashionable Design Inspired
by Your Personal Style

ANNETTE TATUM

Clarkson Potter/Publishers
New York

Copyright © 2009 by Little House
Collections, Inc.

All rights reserved. Published in the
United States by Clarkson Potter/
Publishers, an imprint of the Crown
Publishing Group, a division of
Random House, Inc., New York.
www.crownpublishing.com
www.clarksonpotter.com

CLARKSON POTTER is a trademark
and POTTER with colophon is a
registered trademark of Random
House, Inc.

Library of Congress Cataloging-in-
Publication Data
Tatum, Annette.
    The well-dressed home / Annette
Tatum. — 1st ed.
        p.   cm.
    1. Interior decoration.   I. Title.
NK2115.T32   2009
747—dc22
2008051509

978-0-307-40624-8  2

Printed in China

Design by Jan Derevjanik

10  9  8  7  6  5  4  3  2  1

First Edition

TO MY FAMILY:

Clay, Olivia, Ella, Lena, and Joe

# contents

**PART THREE** | MIXING FASHIONABLE HOME DECOR . . . . . 83

# preface

MY FASCINATION WITH FASHION, AND ESPE-cially with textiles, led to my love of design. When I created my first collection of bedding in 1994, my goal was to encourage design that mixed vintage, traditional, and other styles to create one-of-a-kind interiors. Soon thereafter, I launched House and Little House by Annette Tatum, and Annette Tatum Studio, which have allowed me to incorporate my love of textiles and fashion into home-decor collections.

*The Well-Dressed Home* illustrates my ideas of how to create dynamic interiors by allowing your personal fashion choices to be the inspiration for your home's decor. By using your own fashion style, you will be able to create beautiful rooms that reflect the real you. Like a candid family snapshot, your home will become a layering of the styles you wear and the lifestyle you enjoy.

This book will inspire you to embrace the idea of designing your own home in the same way you choose your day's wardrobe. Your clothing and accessories mirror your unique personality and style, and so should the decor of your home. By using the same style choices used to fashion your wardrobe, you will uncover your own distinctive interior design decor. Your home will become like your wardrobe, a unique, one-of-a-kind expression of you.

THERE HAS BEEN A REVOLUTION IN THE DE-corating world. When past generations made decisions on what their home interiors would look like, their choices were limited. For them, decorating meant little more than choosing a style, such as traditional, Mediterranean, or modern, and selecting a "suite" of matching pieces. Once they committed to a particular style, changing the room was a big deal.

Today, however, stylish furnishings are found everywhere—and not only in designer show-rooms. Department stores, discount outlets, boutiques, and even online sources all tempt you with well-designed goods. These days, shopping for home furnishings can be as exciting, and as much fun, as shopping for clothes.

Clipping items from magazines, watching couture runway shows online, and observing what your favorite movie stars are wearing on the red carpet aren't normally thought of as sources of decorating inspiration, but they're great ways to start. Exploring your own wardrobe is also extremely helpful. Whether the fashions you

prefer are bright or muted, tailored or feminine, casual or formal, they will tell you a great deal about what will make you happiest in the home you're designing.

Since you can often find inspiration in styles you might not wear, or even normally consider, this book highlights eleven popular fashion categories: romantic, couture, classic, casual, bohemian, retro, resort, modern, eclectic, vintage, and eco. For each style, you'll find examples of runway fashions, wardrobe references, and a collage of glorious inspirations. As you flip through the glamorous, refined, fun, and sometimes outrageous photos in the sections that describe these styles, think about what you love about each, and imagine new ways you might use that information to combine colors and textures for your home.

Next, take a look at the rooms that are fea-

tured in this book. You'll notice that some rooms closely parallel specific fashion styles, but most are a mix of several influences. Putting together a wardrobe that relies heavily on one style doesn't mean you can't embellish it with elements from other styles. When you design your home, you have the same freedom.

Translating the many inspirations you've gathered into a workable plan for your home's decor is the most important step in designing a fashionable house. The individual way you interpret or filter your influences into the colors, patterns, furniture, lighting, and accent pieces that make up your home is what produces a look that's all your own.

Often, you can borrow ideas directly from items that inspire you. Sometimes, though, what attracts you to a certain skirt, sheet of gift wrap, or set design of a period reflected in a movie is

more elusive. For example, one room's design (page 151) was inspired by a collection of oil paintings. The owner didn't want to duplicate the exact colors; instead, she reproduced the collection's overall mood.

Many of the rooms in *The Well-Dressed Home* share a spirit of adventure. It takes a leap of faith to let a beaded cashmere cardigan and a pair of flowered sandals fuel a kitchen makeover (page 95), but the results can be sensational. It's equally daring to design a family room that fearlessly combines furnishings inspired by your love of retro modern and your kids' comfort (page 103). These creative fusions prove that incorporating multiple inspirations adds extra depth and interest to your home. For each room in this book, you'll see an explanation of how the various bits and pieces are translated and mixed together to create a pleasing look.

Also in these pages, you'll find a number of collages. Fashion designers call these patchworklike assemblages "storyboards" and use them to organize the ideas that inspire them. The ones here have two purposes. When they illustrate a fashion style, they offer potential ways to translate that style's characteristics into home decorating ideas. When they accompany a home I've featured in the book, the storyboards represent the multifaceted inspirations that led to the design of that particular room.

While there's no one formula for designing a room, a fashion-focused method of decorating will help you borrow from the styles and influences you admire, balance purely decorative items with uniquely personal ones, and create a home that feels right for you and your family. Open up your closet; your guide to designing a well-dressed home awaits you.

PART ONE

# from runway to room

What if when you decorated your home you asked yourself the same question you ask yourself every morning when you get dressed: What do I want to wear today? Putting together a great decorating scheme is actually a similar process to pulling off a fashionable outfit. In fact, inspirations for a terrific-looking home may be right inside your closet.

Since your wardrobe represents the flattering colors, pleasing patterns, and comforting textures you love, why start from scratch when it's time to decorate? Translating your fashion preferences into color palettes, materials, and home furnishings is the first step to creating a more fashionable house.

Think about how you shop for a new outfit. You rarely walk into one store and buy a dress, shoes, and a bag all at once. To create a fashionable home, you need to shop the same way. The couches and table may come from a furniture store, the chairs from an antique dealer, and the lamps from a specialty boutique or a flea market. Take time to gather inspirations that excite you. Look at your favorite fashion and home designers to see whose styles you relate to and admire.

## gathering inspiration

When I start to design a new line of fabrics for my company, I try to look beyond textile references for inspiration. I look at tile patterns, details on old iron gates, unusual architecture, and more. Where do you find inspiration? It might be from fashion magazines, street culture, movies, or architecture.

For me, watching a movie, visiting my favorite store, or going to an opera and taking in set-design elements serves more than one purpose. I love being entertained, but I also get some of my most exciting ideas from the films I watch and the plays I see. The movie *Marie Antoinette,* for example, directed by Sofia Coppola, is a fascinating portrayal of life at Versailles, home of royalty before the French Revolution. While watching the movie, instead of concentrating on the plot, I found myself staring at the opulent decor Coppola conjured up for the party scenes, and fixating on the luxurious ball gowns and towering hairdos she and her designers created for the film's actors. In the silhouettes, patterns, and prints on dazzling display throughout the film, Coppola expertly captured how fashion influenced the lifestyle

and decor of the privileged few in eighteenth-century Versailles, and vice versa.

Have you ever attended a Cirque du Soleil performance? The shows offer a modern take on an old-fashioned one-ring circus. While I always enjoy the performances of this talented troupe for their thought-provoking themes and acrobatic artistry, it's awe-inspiring to see the new design possibilities these artists introduce—using acrobatic motion to create swirls of never-before-seen color combinations and forms. Serendipitous revelations like these, I believe, are the most exciting way to discover design inspirations.

I almost always turn up interesting surprises when I search the Internet. Whether you want to research historical design sources from around the globe or gather inspirations from other communities, other cultures, or other lands, it's out

OPPOSITE AND ABOVE: Betsey Johnson surprises with subtle details, such as sari embroidery on a classic watermelon-colored strapless pouf dress from the 1950s with a flirty furry aqua shrug, while *Vogue* and swatches of fabrics can be the starting point to finding your own inspiration, just as a favorite kimono or piece of comfortable and colorful clothing can be.

there. Where else could you view a collection of gossamer-thin felt gowns from high-fashion Horst Couture of Akron, Ohio, and coquettish separates from Tasmanian-born designer Alannah Hill in the course of ten minutes? You can catch up on Barcelona's street culture or New York's underground art scene without having to get on a plane. You can get a sense of the way in which the creative world is turning, twenty-four hours a day, seven days a week.

Try watching the latest runway collection online, such as *Womenswear Daily*'s www.wwd.com.

Top editors aren't the only ones with access to front-row views of the fashion runways of Paris, Milan, and New York. Now anyone with an Internet connection can instantly see what top designers are offering each season in their spring or fall collections. Online, models from Armani and Christian Dior to Dries Van Noten and Zucca walk the catwalk just for you. Some fashion designers, including Ralph Lauren and Missoni, now offer home collections, too. And while it's always a treat to stroll the aisles at Maison & Objet, the twice-yearly French home furnishings trade show, it's significantly easier to watch the highlights on your computer screen.

Having the world at your fingertips can be exciting, but it can also be daunting. Having too many choices can be overwhelming. That's why I organize notes I've made, pictures clipped from magazines, photographs, swatches of fabrics, and small objects into tangible "style files" (see opposite).

Make a file for each project you want to work on. That way you can add, subtract, and remix your inspirations until you find a combination that works. It really doesn't matter how many different sources you have used as inspiration. What will make the ideas you borrow your own is the way you translate and blend all of the bits and pieces together.

This mood board based with a happy watermelon pink recalls the down-home charm of garden roses, Granny's brooches, and a colorful kaleidoscope of comfy corduroys.

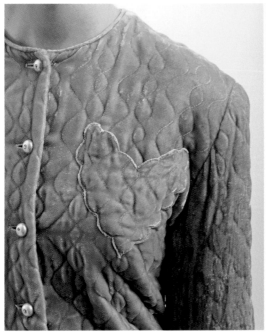

## translating color, pattern, and texture

There are two ways for you to transform your style file into usable decorating ideas: *literal* and *inspirational*. The literal approach is straightforward; it transports the signature spots on a pair of Marc Jacobs ballerina flats or one of his denim totes directly onto an upholstered chair, an area rug, or a lamp shade. The inspirational method, however, translates the silver-gray background and white spots of the flats into a new white and gray color scheme for your bedroom.

Here's another example: by using the literal translation method, you might use the beautiful

way your classic pearl necklace reflects light to create a couture-inspired display of photographs in mother-of-pearl frames, so that you capture that effect in your living room. An inspirational interpretation might prompt you to use pearlized paint on the walls, add a glossy lacquered end table to your bedroom, or reupholster an ottoman in a warm gold and cream print to get the same effect in a somewhat different manner.

### your color palette

Throw open your closet doors. What's your first impression? Do you see a jumble of favorite clothes mixed with seldom-worn items or a tidy, well-organized fashion display? What's important is what you wear, day in and day out.

One of the things I've discovered by looking at the garments in my closet is that there is hardly any plum. If I want to wear a dark hue, I generally wear charcoal, or gray. Since I seldom

ABOVE AND OPPOSITE: The softness of a laundered coral silk velveteen sweater with pearl buttons and a heart appliqué, along with the sparkle of favored beads, pearls, and turquoise rhinestones, can remind us of what colors, textures, and patterns inspire us, as in this dining room with coral and aqua accents.

wear plum, I might hesitate before using it in large proportion in my home. It probably wouldn't be my first choice at a paint store, but since I'm sometimes attracted to patterns with regal purples and plums, I might use these colors for accent items.

Even if I rarely wear certain colors, I'm always open to rethinking my choices and using them in new ways. A fortuitous inspiration might help me to see a certain color in a whole new light. Plum might end up having new possibilities.

What are *your* favorite colors? Many people say blue, but if you look into their clothes closets, there often isn't much blue there. To create rooms as fashionable as you are, identify the colors that dominate your wardrobe. Note the ones that stand out when you take a quick glance.

To create a visual reference of your favorite colors, make a personal fashion profile by taking a series of snapshots, or just set apart all of your pink items from the blues and greens in your closet. In each color section, you'll probably discover varying shades. You'll want to learn whether you prefer light shades (pale periwinkle, perhaps), deep tones (sapphire), or bright ones (azure).

To complete your personal fashion profile, it's essential to know the manner in which you use colors. Do you usually create monochromatic outfits, with belts, purses, and shoes in similar colors, or dress with tiny accent "bursts" featuring several different colors? Are your accessories usually earth tones, romantic pastels, or jewel tones, like ruby, citrine, tourmaline, and amethyst?

One of my clients, who had previously decorated her home for herself, her husband, and daughters, asked me to help her update her house. With her daughters away at college, she wanted to create something grown-up, but not too stylized.

Based on her fairly neutral clothing choices, we outfitted her home with pale-sage sofas, a wood dining table with chairs upholstered in white matelassé, and a bed with a white linen headboard. We then selected two sets of accessories for each room—one in muted woodsy colors to be used as the equivalent of day wear, the other an opulent blend of gem tones for "dress up." In a matter of minutes, new pillows, throws, and a printed lamp shade could change to mirror her mood and newfound direction.

If you share your home with others, as I do, you'll want to pay attention to everyone's likes and dislikes. When you create a home that reflects the tastes of the people you love, you can't go wrong.

## a sense of harmony

While it's important to be aware of your personal colors, it's essential to know how to use them together. Serene, vibrant, harmonious, edgy . . . working with a color wheel can help you select or fine-tune combinations to produce your desired effect.

Color wheels divide colors into two main groups. Warm colors, such as butter yellow and gold, make a room seem cozy and inviting. Cool colors, such as turquoise and sea green, make a space feel refreshing and serene.

OPPOSITE AND RIGHT: Color energizes these Cacharel lace-up wedges that sport Pucci flourishes, while this saturated turquoise and coral home office shows how adding your favorite tones can take the drudgery out of paperwork, and, in fact, make work fun.

COUNTERCLOCKWISE FROM ABOVE RIGHT: Bright coral and crisp white help to make the chore of laundry more cheerful, while patterns in PJs can be downright charming inspiration, as can the rhinestone detailing on a soft cashmere sweater.

Colors opposite each other on the color wheel always provide maximum color contrast (think Valentino red or Schiaparelli pink contrasted with verdant green), while colors located side by side (beige and bronze) provide less contrast. Accenting sunny yellow with lavender creates a more vibrant color combination than one consisting of yellow and peach.

I love using pink as a base when I design.

Depending on the shade you start with, you can make entirely different design statements: a mix of hibiscus pink and tranquil turquoise promises resort-style escape; hot pink mixed with acid green channels childlike memories; and an icy pink shimmers with couture sophistication when combined with gold and silver. While neither gold nor silver is on the color wheel, their sparkle adds interest to any color palette.

My friend Stephanie's favorite wardrobe accent color is a bright coral. So, in Stephanie's laundry room, she contrasted bright cabana coral cabinets with sparkling clean white walls. What better place to use a color that makes you smile than in a room where happiness is usually in short supply?

Let's say red and purple are the basis of your personal color profile and you want to decorate using both hues. You'll soon realize that having the confidence to wear a floor-length full skirt in a scarlet and purple print isn't nearly as daring as decorating your entire living room in these intense tones. When used on a large scale, some color combos are overpowering. Try toning down one of the two colors and replace the pure red with a rose pink. The effect is both subtler and more livable. Even colors that don't normally work well together often look great when less intensified.

Jewelry can offer new and exciting color combinations. Check out traditional costumes in foreign films, museum costume exhibits, and photos of exotic travel destinations and you'll soon learn that color is perceived differently around the world.

## the power of color

Many people use color to accentuate their body's assets and disguise less-than-perfect proportions. I've always been amazed at how wearing the same color on both top and bottom can make you look taller, how tops with horizontal stripes create the illusion of a more ample bosom, and how white pants make skinny legs look fuller.

The same fool-the-eye tricks work in our homes. Painting adjoining rooms in matching or similar colors appears to expand square footage. Stripes make narrow rooms appear wider, and white spaces feel larger overall. If you dress in black to slim your silhouette, that trick can't be transferred to your home—it really isn't a good idea to decorate your home entirely in black. Instead, use dark browns, greens, or blues (paired with lighter furniture and accent pieces) to make cavernous rooms look cozier.

By using warm and cool colors correctly you can direct attention where you want it. Warm tones from the red-yellow-orange side of the color wheel draw the eye forward. Cool ones, such as blue, green, and purple, tend to recede into the background. You can use these contrary qualities to square off a long, narrow room by painting the two short walls a warmer shade than the two long ones. Or if you discover that your old sofa looks overly large in your new house, you can make it look more in proportion with the room by slipcovering it in a cool shade and painting the wall behind it in a similar cool shade. Pastel and other low-intensity furnishings appear to back away, creating the illusion of more space.

Choosing a single color or similar colors can make a maze of small spaces, or two adjacent ones (such as a kitchen and breakfast nook), appear unified. This ploy also creates a better visual flow in areas that can be viewed from a common vantage point, such as a staircase, and ties together transitional walls like hallways.

Strong colors or high-contrast ones can create focal points on a garment *or* in a room. The contrasting trim is what makes a Chanel jacket so unique. Consider translating this classic concept into your home by allowing pale moldings and railings to stand out against darker walls.

High-intensity colors, such as eye-popping daffodil yellow, party pink, and cobalt blue, appear to jump out at you. These attention-getting colors can be employed as unexpected decorative accents. Bright colors can also be used to lure the eye to specific parts of a room and away from other areas.

## your pattern profile

Borrowing colors from your personal palette and bringing them into your home is a surefire way to feel at ease with your surroundings. But picking the right colors isn't enough; you need to consider patterns, too.

There are times when I substitute my usual white T-shirt for a strong, floral-print blouse; I simply want a little change of scenery. And there are times when I set our dinner table with my favorite turquoise tablecloth, the one that has wood-block prints of white peonies—it makes an ordinary school night less mundane and adds some "pep" to dinnertime. Patterns have a way of changing the ordinary into the extraordinary.

Patterns can sometimes create a mood even more dramatically than colors by referencing a historical era, displaying a foreign sensibility, creating a natural aura, or alluding to your whimsical side. Combining appropriate patterns allows you to re-create, with surprising accuracy, a French château, a surfer's bungalow, or a cozy 1940s kitchen.

Since trendy motifs often fall from favor as quickly as the seasons change, a decor that relies too heavily on them may soon look dated. I prefer to use patterns as accents in a room, not as a main theme. This way, when distinctive designs seem "so last year," it's easy to switch to a new look with minimal effort.

If you're comfortable wearing patterns, it's easy to transfer your favorite motifs directly from your wardrobe to your home. The same tartan plaids and leafy prints that fashion designers often use are also available in upholstery-weight fabric and wallpaper patterns. You can also re-create patterns you love using stenciled borders or tiled murals along wall and ceiling edges.

Are you pattern-shy? Stylized flowers on a Stella McCartney dress you admire but don't often wear might motivate you to find a coverlet in a monochromatic floral. Subtle patterning, such as the swirls on a moiré silk blouse, can reappear as waterlike ripples in a molded-glass countertop. And if your pattern tolerance is especially low, the simplicity of a classic ticking stripe will add subtle changes to your room. A soft stripe pattern

OPPOSITE AND ABOVE: In this bedroom, swirling patterns of pink and orange paisley lend a 1970s joie de vivre, while the pink-and-white tartan carpet is a more grounding force. Girls Rule! offers the same nod to 1970s chic in their fearless coat while Blumarine grounds the rich turquoise and acid pink in this dress. Brown offers an earthy contrast to the garden floral tones on this antique settee and wallpaper, both patterned with bold flowers.

on a sofa in low-contrast colors blends rather than calls attention to itself.

## it's in the mix

Unlike couture creations, ready-to-wear garments tend to limit the number of patterns featured in a single outfit. Outlandish combinations no woman in her right mind would wear in public get media attention—but harmonious outfits actually sell. It's all a matter of wearability.

In a well-dressed home, confrontational patterns certainly make a strong decorating statement, but the resulting environment isn't necessarily visually pleasant. To design livable rooms, interior designers balance patterns in terms of color, scale, and magnitude.

Mixing patterns is an art, but it's one that is worth mastering. Choosing patterns that share the same color family is a key to success. Whenever I visit my friend Claudia, I head straight to her pool house—not because I can't wait to take a dip in the pool, but because I delight in her daring combination of Missoni prints on the umbrellas, deck chairs, pillows, and towels. Even her floor is a mosaic of marine shades of marble. As if reflecting the Pacific Ocean, which is just a few steps from her back door, the patterns form a kaleidoscope of sparkling blues and greens.

Managing the scale of the patterns in a room is important, too. A large-scale Marimekko pattern looks wonderful on a wall or folding screen, but using the same pattern to upholster a chair can be excessive. I like to limit a room's overall color palette if I plan on using large-scale patterns. This keeps the broad lines from overwhelming everything else in the room.

If patterns are your passion, a room with numerous Florence Broadhurst or Lilly Pulitzer prints can be appealing. Simply surround each dominant design with an attention-getting solid color. Using this principle, I have been able to break the widely accepted "no more than three patterns in a room" rule and get great results.

## texture perception

Texture affects the way clothes feel (silky, rough, or soft) and how they look. It's what makes wearing a taffeta skirt a sensuous sensation or a fleece jacket feel cuddly. Texture also adds to the way a well-dressed room "feels."

Your choice of textures in a room allows visitors to quickly know how comfortable they should feel in this part of your home. Cozy chenille couches invite guests to come and hang out, while tight, smooth wool sofas signal that this is a place for more formal interactions. Soft surfaces, like a comfy cable-knit sweater, feel friendly, while hard ones, like a minimalist black turtleneck, are perceived as "for grown-ups only."

Textures beg to be touched. Run your hands across the items in your closet. How do they feel? What is the ratio of matte surfaces to sparkling ones? Do you wear mainly clothes with a silky hand or those with soft natural fibers?

Textures used in apparel fabrics, such as nubs, slubs, bouclés, and chenille, are now frequently found in interior design. Upholstery fabrics tend to have smoother weaves because they can withstand more wear, but don't overlook bolts of bouclé-type fabrics, which can add texture to decorative accents.

Including texture in your decorating schemes is especially important when your color palette is monochromatic. Imagine, for a minute, a room in which everything is white. If it's decorated with loosely woven linen, white denim, and sailcloth, it becomes a space with a casual air. But substitute cut velvet, satin, and damask fabrics and you've got a room with a more formal look. Finally, exchange those textures for silk, satin, organza, and lace and your imaginary room is filled with romance.

Fabrics aren't the only way you can create texture in your home. Paint finishes, intricate

OPPOSITE AND ABOVE: Mermaid texture reigns in a powder-blue curvy wedge; textured trims of beads, straw, and rope; Zac Posen's metallic shift of scales; and in the wavy wood detailing on the ceiling of this otherwise understated and classic dining room.

moldings, brick, stone, furniture, and carpet pile also extend the range of materials available to you. Details such as crown moldings, faux-textured paints, and decorative ceiling treatments all help to create texture in a room, too.

## contrast counts

Renaissance brocades edged with silk ruffles, gold lamé accented with semisheer sequins, fluid knits trimmed with opulent fur . . . runway fashions revel in textural contrasts. Pairing high-contrast materials like metal chains and embossed emblems with leather makes designer handbags look exciting. Combining items with similar textures, like satiny charmeuse and

lustrous glissenette, results in a more demure statement for lingerie.

I often create interesting surface tensions when I design a new product line for my company or a new look for my home. I pair velvet with satin for a soft-versus-sleek effect, and pleat fabric to form three-dimensional ruffles and rosettes that can be added to flat window coverings and lamp shades. Quilting is also a great way to create monochromatic textures on furniture.

Positioning hard materials like metal and glass near soft ones such as plush pillows and billowing drapes sets up your home's basic textural contrast. Complementing shiny surfaces with matte ones creates visual excitement. Bohemian-style rooms can be layered with tile patterns from around the world. Rooms with a retro vibe frequently revel in combinations of glossy plastics and natural materials.

Sharp contrasts in texture demand special attention. Shag rugs or ultrathick wool Flokatis on a smooth floor act as an exclamation point to highlight the floor's beauty. But combining items with similar textures results in a quieter statement. Pairing dissimilar textures in the same color family makes for a pleasing compromise.

Using contrasting paint finishes on your walls and moldings creates subtle texture. For the walls, flat paint offers a lusterless surface, while eggshell or satin paints have just a hint of sheen. Sand-textured and stucco paints provide the roughest surfaces. For the moldings, gloss adds a shiny coat. Faux finishes, such as sponging, combing, and trompe l'oeil (which means

OPPOSITE AND ABOVE: The vibrancy of high-contrast black and white with a hit of citron keeps this entry hall and Antonio Beradi ensemble fresh, despite the use of traditional details, such as the wallpaper and antiques in the interior and the ruffles and eyelet in the fashion.

"to fool the eye"), use color to trick you into seeing textures, such as wood graining and stone, where they don't actually exist. Mixing contrasting elements in a room, such as smooth, rough, shiny, or matte, is one of the things that makes a room interesting. Balancing contrast creates beauty and depth, allowing the eye to weave easily throughout the room's space.

## details matter

What makes an Armani dress so much more special than a bargain-rack suit? It's the details. Detailing is what you notice first when you look at antique or high-end clothing. Smocking, ruching, wrinkling, and gathering, along with added-on embellishments like tassels, jewels, and trim, recall more gracious times when most items were lovingly handcrafted and beautifully ornamented.

Enhancing the furnishings you already own can make plain or mass-produced items look one of a kind. Aim for a grand effect worthy of a couture collection using add-ons like hand-tied tassels, scalloped silk trims, and Austrian Swarovski crystals, or create a simple spark of interest by adding contrasting piping to a window-seat cushion, attaching a satin box pleat edging to a linen lamp shade, or stitching fabric flowers folded like origami to a pillow top.

In the world of *passementerie* (French for "trimmings"), the high-end embellishments of Scalamandré stand out. Cinch a drapery panel with one of their tasseled cords and your window will surely get a second look. Encircle an ottoman with one of their ball or bullion fringes and you've created a piece of furniture that is no longer a mere footnote to its larger companion.

Since trimmings are, in essence, jewelry for your home, I sometimes raid my jewelry box and use the beautiful things I bought to adorn myself to make my furniture beautiful instead. A vintage brooch can not only be worn but also pinned to a curtain, a pillow, or a table runner you want to dress up in a special way.

To provide a yin and yang sense of balance to the feminine tiaras and feathery plumes in your home's decor, borrow cuff links, tie clips, and bow ties from your husband's haberdashery drawer: not all details need to be frilly. Do you

like the way starched white collars and cuffs "pop" a blue oxford shirt? Then why not trim a bed skirt with crisp white shirting fabric?

Just as the accessories you choose to wear depend on the event to which you are going, the details you add to a room depend on the way you use your room. Obviously, you'll want to be more daring in your choice of shoes when you're on a Caribbean vacation than when you're getting dressed for a business meeting.

Sometimes, in both dressing and decorating, it's smart to play it safe, and sometimes taking risks is the right thing to do. What's important is to be honest with yourself about how "out there" you are willing to be. If you have always been timid about adding color to your

home, start small before committing to a new bold palette. It isn't a big deal to buy a wild print scarf, then decide you've made a mistake; but buying a sofa in a pattern you'll quickly regret can be costly. Only you can decide whether the rewards outweigh the risks.

Of course, decorating isn't always about *your* comfort zone. When you choose an outfit for yourself, you're the only one who has to live with the consequences—but when you redecorate your home, your whole family has to live with your design choices. When there's a houseful of children and pets to take into account, practicality often wins out over high design.

If some of your ideas are met with skepticism from your loved ones, don't give up. Follow

OPPOSITE AND ABOVE: Beautiful details, such as the perfect roll on the chiffon cap sleeves and just enough ruffling in this Behnaz Sarafpour dress, the velvet and contrast of textured piping in this row of pumps, or an impeccable row of bronze-finished tacks in this George Smith upholstered chair, are what draw our attention to good design, both for our wardrobe and our homes.

your heart in your private domains, but make compromises in the rooms everyone shares. Take pleasure in how terrific your walk-in closet, pantry, or home office looks, and help your family to understand your inspirations for your new decor. Encourage them to identify their own tastes in fashion and you'll be pleasantly surprised at how quickly your well-dressed house will emerge.

# design style guide

THIS STYLE GUIDE SUMMARIZES THE "LOOK" FOR ELEVEN POPULAR FASHION CATEGORIES: ROMANTIC, COUTURE, CLASSIC, CASUAL, BOHEMIAN, RETRO, RESORT, MODERN, ECLECTIC, VINTAGE, AND ECO.

Delve into each design style, taking notes as you go. Imagine the influences each style might have on the rooms in your home. Which styles do you most identify with, in both your wardrobe and your house? Even if you aren't personally familiar with the patterns, fabrics, colors, and designers that are iconic to these styles, consider what it would be like to blend the ones that you are drawn to into your living room, bedroom, hallway, and even the alcoves in your home. In Part III, you'll see these design styles in action to further inspire.

So break down any self-imposed fashion or home-design boundaries you have, mix and match, open up, and have fun. A fashionable home that expresses your personal style is well within reach.

Here's a quick reference guide of the characteristics for each design style found in the style guide:

ROMANTIC . soft, pale, pink lingerie, roses

COUTURE . . lavish, elegant, exquisite, decadent, one of a kind

CLASSIC . . . polo, New York, equestrian, worldly, antique, tailored

CASUAL . . . comfy, easy, faded

BOHEMIAN . worldly, well-traveled, gypsy, colorful

RETRO . . . . yesterday, hip, nostalgic

RESORT . . . fresh, island life, light, breezy

MODERN . . sleek, minimal, high design, functional

ECLECTIC . . mix and match, layered, inventive

VINTAGE . . treasure, sparkle, satin, nostalgic

ECO . . . . . . simple, green, recycled, clean

# romantic

ROMANTIC STYLE IS LIKE POETRY IN MOTION. It evokes music through visible rhythms of fabrics falling in soft curves, teasing hints of color, and patterns that inspire longing. Sometimes innocent, sometimes seductive, it celebrates the desire to be with the one who makes your heart beat faster or the yearning for romance.

Inspired by on-screen lovers like Shakespeare's Romeo and Juliet, a dreamy wedding party, or even fairy tales, romantic style embraces your softer side. No two interpretations of this style are exactly alike. Romance, like beauty, is in the eye of the beholder.

Fabrics that appeal to both the eye and the touch are one of the hallmarks of this enchanting style. Anna Molinari's fluffy angora cardigans, clingy jersey skirts, and silky slip dresses make Blumarine creations a thrill to handle. Kate and Laura Mulleavy, the California sisters behind the Rodarte label, show their romantic bent on the runway with sheer tea-party florals and frothy tiers of organza. And few designers embrace romance like Alannah Hill, Australia's leading purveyor of flirty tactile confections.

Shying away from neutrals, the romantic color palette flirts with dreamy pastels of pink while inviting darker shades that tempt with subtle hints. Take reds, for example. The most voluptuous color family includes the palest blush tones, amorous pinks, and siren scarlet. Both reds and pinks denote love, but while reds are like a love letter that boldly declares passion, pinks whisper with affection.

For a passionate color pair, marry garden-inspired greens with demure whites, such as heirloom ivory, fragrant jasmine, and English cream. If those aren't your color preferences, try quiet blues and muted whites, like the ones found in traditional Wedgwood pottery, which is a classic romantic color combination.

Romantic details are meant to make you feel as beautiful as you look. Whether you prefer traditional flourishes that recall old-style femininity or today's more modern approach to romance, it's easy to translate the sweet qualities of romantic style that you admire into your home's design.

Inspired by the colors of your favorite Chloé print dress, you might design your home's guest room to resemble an opulent Fabergé egg, using a palette of blushing rose, innocent lilacs, sky blues, and celadon greens. If your shoes, skirts, or jewelry reflect richer, saturated colors, however, you might choose ruby red, sapphire blue, or emerald green as the heart of your color scheme. A room decorated in these gemlike tones will feel as romantic as a jeweled choker. Both of these looks are as romantic as they are fabulous.

Like the beautiful lingerie you wear under your clothes, your bedroom is personal and private. It's where you can indulge in small luxuries or splurge on a hand-carved European antique bed, soft and luxurious linens, and deep down-filled cushions. Designing an elegant and sensual look entirely in romantic white can conjure up that bridal feeling.

Billowing fabrics, an aesthetic beloved by fashion designers, can also add romance to your home in the shape of fluttering window treatments, poufed bed skirts, or bubble-hem tablecloths. Consider the way that sheer linen

panels hung from the tester of a four-poster bed imparts a wonderfully intimate feeling. The air of secrecy or lightly veiled privacy the panels create transforms a functional piece of furniture into a serene sanctuary.

Vintage textiles, such as tea-stained lace, cabbage-rose chintz, and toile de Jouy illustrated with scenes of courting couples and summer picnics, lend an amorous ambience to your retreat. If you want a sophisticated look rather than a sweet one, balance patterned fabrics with a generous amount of solid ones, such as lingerie satin and cashmere.

Whether fairy-tale pretty, sleek and sophisticated, or spirited and edgy, the romantic-style space creates an illusion that everything in it—functional or decorative—has been selected for no other purpose than to bring you the feeling of a heartfelt home.

OPPOSITE AND ABOVE: Delicate sea pearls surrounding gleaming amethyst stones hand-wired in rose gold provide romantic shimmer to a wardrobe or room, while the floaty organdy dress fashioned in layers pairs elegantly with balle-rina details and grosgrain ribbon. All of these surfaces combine to create an interesting romantic palette of textures and hues easily transferable to a room.

Pair
110" x 59"

78¼" x 53"

*Curtains should break ½" to 1" on the floor.*
—Miles Redd

# couture

COUTURE STYLE IMPARTS AN AIR OF INDUL-
gence. It takes the best of everything to the next
level, revels in fantasies of opulence, and delights
in decadent excess. Too much is never enough.
Formal by nature, extravagantly elegant, and
voluptuously layered, this over-the-top style
demands attention.

With its roots in the nineteenth century,
haute couture is the pampered child of Parisian
society. This exclusive coterie of designers spe-
cializes in creating custom apparel with the
finest fabrics and workmanship that is beyond
compare. The House of Dior's luxe silks, brocades, and damasks are embellished with tiny
beads, pearls, and jewels for a royal semblance.
Philippine-born designer Monique Lhuillier's
voluminous draping and gathering of gossamer
cloth into a single evening dress is guaranteed
to make the wearer stand out in a crowd. And
the centerpiece of Prada's atelier collection are
garments dripping in flamboyant lace, gold, and
crystals. As much as couture shouts drama,
it retains its cachet because its effervescent

43

"Couture style of the privileged few is attainable by all—even if only in the confines of your own bedroom."

CLOCKWISE FROM BELOW: Christian Dior's Paris haute couture collection channels old-world courtly glamour with new-world colors of pale chartreuse fading into an earthy taupe peplum. Accessories such as hand-wired pearl-and-crystal tiaras, channel-cut diamonds, and opalescent sequined slippers can be a point of departure for accessorizing your home.

qualities are rare. Surrounding yourself with objects created with the utmost care for you alone is the soul of couture.

Couture colors flash like precious metals and gleam like gems. A flattering custom palette is a significant part of the couture mystique. Colors should be chosen with care, because ivory, moss green, and blush pink might be pleasing for some, but these pastels infused with a hint of beige or gray might be more becoming for you.

What would a room look like if your diamond ring inspired it? Imagine all the ways you could add sparkling subtleties to a monochromatic palette of platinum, silver, smoke, and shimmering grays.

The couture home exhibits the same design principles that fashion houses have always used: precision tailoring, lavish custom-crafted details, and a sense of pampered elegance. The style embraces eighteenth-century European royal court dress, subjected to the nips and tucks of a twenty-first-century sensibility.

Marie Antoinette was legendary for transferring her sumptuous taste in clothing to her living quarters. At Versailles everything was executed with exquisite workmanship. Even the window locks and doorknobs were, and still are, miniature masterpieces. Like the awe-inspiring Hall of Mirrors at Versailles, today's couture home sparkles when its design elements re-create real or faux polished marble, crystal chandeliers, and silver candelabra.

Couture fashion collections are well known for creating a sense of excitement through accessories. Over-the-top jewels, tiaras, feathered headpieces, and beaded bags often steal the spotlight from the apparel on display. You can create the same buzz in your home. Layer an aristocratic sash across the back of a chair or crown a pillow with an antique brooch. You might even edge palatial drapes with jeweled fringe, regal braid, or golden tassels to create a look that is positively Baroque.

Inspired by the luminous strands of pearls in your jewelry box, you might want to experiment with pearlized paint, a lustrous liquid that gives walls and furniture a beautiful pearly finish. On a smaller scale, why not capture the effect pearls have on a black dress by displaying a collection of opalescent mother-of-pearl vases on a black ebony sideboard?

Couture style of the privileged few is attainable by all—even if only in the confines of your own bedroom.

Using fantasy and extravagance as the basis of your couture-style home's decor, you can mix basic elements from different periods and styles without regard to conventional design restrictions. Add just a few dazzling touches or transform your space with layers of specifically placed details throughout your well-dressed home. Depending on your tastes and budget, your couture-style home may curtsy deeply to the great homes and palaces of the past or simply give a majestic nod toward extravagant design.

# classic

CLASSIC STYLE IS TIMELESS, NOT TRENDY. It's the gentleman dressed in a navy blue blazer at the polo match. With elements alluding to an Ivy League ancestry, stately English manor homes, and yachting regattas, this style relies on an enduring vision of timeless beauty and distinction.

Steeped in history but not nostalgic, this style is always discreet and well mannered, never loud or inappropriate. In our fickle society, few things are meant to last forever; that's what makes classic style so remarkable. Like Jay Gatsby's fondness for polo ponies, lawn parties, and pocket watches, the familiar textures, traditional silhouettes, and crisp colors keep classic style feeling comfortable and reassuring.

While today's trendy styles are outdated in a matter of months, and tomorrow's must-haves are passé before you've paid off your credit-card balance, a classic design exudes a self-assured quality. Each neatly pressed trouser, Newport polo shirt, or ascot by Ralph Lauren is perennially stylish. Oscar de la Renta's creations, whether custom-designed for a First Lady, Mummy's garden party, or a future CEO, always look classy and refined without seeming ostentatious. It's hard to imagine an era when a Chanel jacket would feel out of date.

Understated but far from boring, the classic color palette revolves around basic black, white, cream, gray, navy, red, hunter green, and brown. Shades inspired by nature's unchanging matter—quarried stone, trees, and mountain ranges—impart a sense of stability.

The style's essential color combinations mix a trio of monochromatic neutrals: a light tone to catch the eye, a dark one for depth, and a third in a medium shade to provide balance. For example, the contrast between baby blue and saturated midnight might be moderated with opaque cornflower, pale silver and dusky charcoal can be softened with fox gray, and cream spiked with dark espresso can be mellowed with khaki.

Visual discretion, a cornerstone of classic style, is championed in signature fabrics, such as wool gabardine, Belgian linen, and cotton twills. Patterns, when used, tend to be subtle. Tweeds, basket weaves, pinstripes, plaids, and houndstooth checks never scream "Look at me"; instead they play a supporting role.

More than any other factor, the contrast of rough and soft textures gives classic style its stately feeling. A medley of luxuriously supple wool and cashmere throws can be your home's equivalent of an angora evening stole. Softness is an invitation to linger. Who can resist the urge to settle down in a worn leather club chair when it's adorned with a Pendleton plaid blanket.

In the same way a tasteful belt or a single overcast seam can serve as the focal point of a Bill Blass dress, a classic-style room is designed with attention to practical details. Sofas, chairs, and headboards upholstered in functional, not fancy, fabrics or naturally tanned leathers impart a cozy

Classic details for wardrobe and home include the whip-stitching of a Tod's driving moc, piles of pearls, and a tweedy wool bouclé à la legendary classics creator Coco Chanel.

club atmosphere against a dignified backdrop. In the dining room of the classic-style home, an antique mahogany table is always polished to a mirror shine and silver is for everyday use.

Walls painted in shades of gray flannel can be kicked up a notch with textured finishes resembling antique leather, brushed suede, or pebbly river rocks. Or opt out of neutrals altogether and choose a more color-heavy palette with shades borrowed from tartan plaids or the stripes painted on a vintage croquet set.

Since a classic-style home must be stylish yet sensible, interior woodwork is typically of a practical nature. Chair or plate rails are fine, decorative corbels less so. Traditional flooring materials such as hardwood, marble, or stone tile will give the look a solid base. Oriental rugs are indispensable, not just because they introduce an extra layer of pattern to a classic room but also because they make any space feel warmer.

Tastefully arranged collectibles have a similar effect. Inspired by French designer Christian Audigier's argyle patterns and royal emblems, play up your love of cuff links with props covered in harlequin diamonds and faux family crests. Or declare your thoroughbred status by displaying vintage riding gear such as an Hermès saddle.

Of course, if you don't want your home to look like a stage set for a period drama, it's a good idea to break character with a few vibrant or trendy accents. Imagine the stir you'd create by wearing stiletto heels or clutching a red patent leather purse with a Burberry or Akiko Ogawa trench coat. Placing a modern sculpture on an antique campaign chest has the same effect.

There's no question that classic style benefits from adding your own quirky perspective because it's a time-tested formula. So don't shy away from what's accepted and expected; instead add your personal monogram. It may be just the right time to reacquaint yourself with the classics.

# casual

CASUAL STYLE PUTS COMFORT ABOVE ALL else. Wear your hair in a ponytail, put your feet on the coffee table, drink your morning coffee at two in the afternoon: living a casual lifestyle is like having a month of Sundays.

Being casual frees you from formal rules. Surfers, pop stars, and off-season sports heroes are this style's media icons. A carefree attitude, not tradition, is what matters most. With a soundtrack of chill-out vibes, easy-listening tunes, or Bruce Springsteen, the relaxed lifestyle appeals to your inner child.

Today's interpretation of casual style is polished and sophisticated. Michael Kors's sassy Capri-inspired stripes are found on everything from his luxury T-shirt dresses to his soothing bedding collections. Lacoste, the French apparel company known for its green crocodile logo, offers fashion-forward sportswear, watches, and purses. And Calvin Klein brings his casual-style ethic to the runway with trendy jeans, oversized sweaters, and provocative, yet practical, underwear.

51

The casual color palette can be found in the sand and sea of coastal California, where weekends are for skiing or snowboarding in the mountains, or simply relaxing in your garden. Choosing a color scheme is easy. Blues, yellows, and greens are perennial favorites, and they look fresh and breezy in sun-bleached shades. In brighter hues, they take on a nautical feel.

Create an ode to summer inspired by croquet and wide canvas awnings with lemon, lime, and navy stripes. Pretend every day is the Fourth of July on Nantucket by combining red, white, and blue. Use tennis whites, sage, and khaki for neutral colors. And nothing says casual like a mix of laid-back blues.

When comfort is your top priority in clothing, why not let that same comfort spill over into your home's design? Overstuffed sofas and chairs can be as relaxed as unstructured jackets and relaxed pants. Modest textiles like muslin, twill, denim, and ticking are nice choices for casual upholstery. White cotton slipcovers always feel casual and are extremely child- and pet-friendly. Toss them in the washer, add a little bleach, and they come out looking good as new.

Just as a stylish, casual outfit can consist of only a T-shirt, khakis, and slip-on shoes, a house in which the furnishings have been pared down feels more relaxed than one that is cluttered. Avoid loading your mantel with photographs or your coffee table with odds and ends. Simplify things with a big container of garden greens and a fresh mood will be set.

Keep patterns understated and to a mini-

mum. Contrasts between design motifs and fabric or wall-covering backgrounds should be subtle. Stripes, however, are an exception. Take advantage of the distinctive lines in tongue-and-groove wainscot paneling or striped wall coverings. High-contrast awning stripes are perfect for upholstering outdoor furniture or indoor accent pieces.

As with a Marc Jacobs Aran cable pullover or a Prada smocked-bodice sundress, textures, not patterns, add interest to casual decor. Pair rough surfaces with smooth ones. Toss bulky knit pillows onto flat jersey duvets. Layer your table with a ripstop tablecloth overlaid with a slubby linen runner, then add mix-and-match chairs with distressed paint.

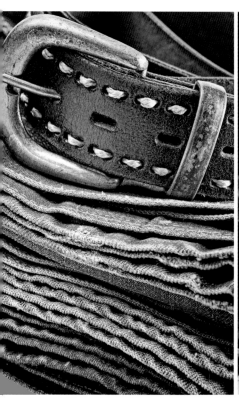

A casual home thrives on light, so keep window coverings to a minimum. If going bare isn't possible, forgo anything fussy or multi-layered. Easygoing roll-up Roman shades in voile or sheer lawn fabric are more in character. Tab-top curtains or those that tie on to a simple drapery rod look less formal than traditional drapery headings.

While there will always be those who lament the lack of formality in our society, casual style is here to stay. If you're wondering whether your home feels casually chic, get dressed in your best weekend wear, then walk from room to room. Do you feel as if you fit in? If your answer is yes, you've achieved casual style.

OPPOSITE AND ABOVE: Beat-up canvas Jack Purcell Converse lace-up tennis shoes, blue denim jeans with a character-building leather belt, nautical stripes and eyelet from Michael Kors, and a pair of periwinkle-piped PJs all say casual, comfortable, and perennially hip for both the wearer and the decorator.

# bohemian

MULTICULTURAL AND MULTIETHNIC, BOHEMIAN style is a boisterous caravan of color. Patchwork patterns and layers of exotic texture flaunt non-conformity as a badge of honor.

To a bohemian, the correct choice when given multiple options is "all of the above." There are no wrong answers, only possibilities to explore. Past, present, and future merge into a whirlwind fusion. Not for the timid, bohemian style (boho for short) is your passport to adventure.

Mixing a little of this and a little of that is a big part of bohemian style. In the sixties and seventies, British designer Thea Porter infused her harem-inspired caftans with an artful pastiche of embellished fabrics from the Upper Nile, medieval England, and the czar's Russian court. Today, Anna Sui earns her boho credentials with dresses inspired by Janis Joplin's signature iridescent hues. Christian Lacroix's atelier whips up flamboyant evening wear that is equal parts French chic, Haight-Ashbury, and Moroccan souk.

"Colors from a Balinese puppet show, an Andean poncho, or a nomadic woven camel saddle are part of the boho quest."

CLOCKWISE FROM TOP RIGHT: The Far East, with India as the star, is the basis of this bohemian spirit. Like a magpie decorates its nest with sparkly bits and pieces found all around, the bohemian decorates one's body with beaded slippers, shimmering saris, armfuls of bangles, and a riot of color, as shown in Blumarine's heavily patterned and embroidered runway look, which manages to appear as light as a feather.

A medley of spicy colors, sunny jewel tones, and earthy hues, the boho palette is flush with patterns. When borrowing shades of mustard, persimmon, and cinnamon from a Silk Road carpet, the color recipe alone might not tell the whole story. You may also want to interpret the rug's ethnic motifs through your own alluring blend.

Bohemian style in the home comes in both bright hues and rich dark tones. Put together palettes with shades that suggest exotic quests. Colors from a Balinese puppet show, an Andean poncho, or a nomadic woven camel saddle are part of the boho quest. You might reach back to bohemian style's heyday in the 1960s. Reimagine the psychedelic clothing worn by the hippie generation for a countercultural twist.

Today's nomadic spirit decorates the home with a global view. Pair a multicolored tablecloth that resembles a flounced Armani gypsy skirt with a chandelier bedecked with jangling pendant "earrings" for a distinctive dining room. Teaming up saffron-tinted silk curtains from India, an embroidered pillow from Japan, and an ikat-dyed mat from Turkey also works.

When choosing bohemian elements for your home, build fashionable character with textures and details. In the same way Luella Bartley, the New York design darling, winds embroidery and braid around her creations' hemlines, use brocade ribbons for trimming an ottoman. Make sure every part of your room offers the eye something to admire, from clever craftsmanship to a wealth of embellishment. Use patterns on your walls, floors, rugs, furniture, and ceramics to create a breathtaking sensory overload.

With air travel making the planet smaller all the time, it's not unusual for travelers to want to re-create a specific feeling or ethnic atmosphere in their own corner of the world. You might design a sumptuous at-home getaway in a spare room by piling plush cushions on a daybed, and stacking a nearby table with well-read books and photographs from distant places.

In the same way a lavish assortment of necklaces and rings can turn an ordinary outfit into a bohemian ensemble, the right accessories can turn a nook into a mini retreat. Hang a hammock or drape lengths of gold-edged sari fabric from the ceiling to cosset a comfy chair, pull up a low Moroccan-style table, and you're on your way to a new destination.

Developing a bohemian style doesn't require a particular visa, international airfare, or formal plans. Surrounding yourself with treasures that have been embellished by hand—block-printed fabrics, wood surfaces inlaid with colored stones, and tiles hand-painted with a labyrinth of intricate motifs—offers a link to other cultures, exotic locales, and other people. If something attracts your eye, it doesn't matter where it is from or what it's made of; go for it. Nurture your wanderlust and design your home as if you live in a nomadic enclave or a maharaja's palace, and suddenly your bohemian fantasies will feel closer to reality.

# retro

RETRO STYLE TAKES ITS ROOTS FROM THE past while still being relevant to the moment. Constantly evolving with time, it offers different meanings and references to every generation. Filtered through a hip time capsule of innovative color and design, retro jives to a jazz beat, gyrates to Elvis, swoons over Sinatra.

Sip a pink cocktail poured from a stainless-steel martini shaker while sitting on an Eames chair in your midcentury ranch home. Take a road trip in a gleaming silver Airstream. This optimistic style's unprecedented creativity erases the lines between fashion, fine art, and industrial design. Form follows function. It's hot to be cool.

Retro designers rely on avant-garde patterns to convey the spirit of this dynamic era. Miu Miu, Prada's youth-centric line, reinvents seventies geometric prints. Finnish-based Marimekko clones A-line dresses in the bright poppies and florals that brought them their original fame.

To make a strong visual connection with a specific time period, a true retro palette should feature an authentic combination of color shades: bubble-gum pink and hot red for the 1950s; bright orange, moody olive, and mustard yellow for the 1960s; white, black, and cement gray for the 1970s; and disco purple and neon everything for the 1980s. Shared palettes offer deep distinctions, as seen in the vibrant orange and olive hues of an Emilio Pucci caftan and the earthy brown, tan, and orange of a Pierre Cardin pantsuit.

To create a retro room, borrow a recipe from Fiesta, Hall, and LuRay kitchen pottery and blend periwinkle, persimmon, and surf green into a nostalgic look that's easy on the eyes. Check out classic car colors, too. Imagine painting your kitchen the color of a pink Cadillac with lemon and lime accents or sitting down for breakfast at a sleek chrome table. Stride along a checkerboard linoleum floor inspired by the white interior trim and black vinyl roof of a classic Ford Mustang. The set of colors you choose will be determined by the era that most appeals to you.

Like the patterned shift dresses favored by Jacqueline Kennedy during her husband's presidential campaign, retro fashion hints are simplified and fun. Florals are stylized; free-form shapes look like amoebas; and multi-colored geometric sticks, squares, and dots are grounded by solid backdrops. Polynesian motifs and barkcloth fabrics tout tiki culture and tropical blooms. A guest room decorated in these

"The set of colors you choose will be determined by the era that most appeals to you."

pop patterns somehow feels both retro and totally modern.

Architectural elements influence all spheres of retro aesthetics. Pierre Cardin's famous bubble dress is built on a unisphere. Isamu Noguchi's cylinder lamps and Arne Jacobsen's egg chairs forecast limitless design possibilities. Today, you can create a retro decor with original pieces found at vintage shops and boutiques specializing in this period or newly minted classics. Many classic twentieth-century icons have never gone out of production. Charles and Ray Eames's lounge chair and ottoman and George Nelson's ball clock are still cutting-edge examples of product design.

Like Mrs. Robinson's leopard-print jacket and patterned shift dresses in *The Graduate,* the film's sets of California homes capture that era's groovy vibe. Success and financial wealth, as a character in the film advises Dustin Hoffman, boils down to one word: "Plastics." Not withstanding the irony inherent in the comment, this cheap and endlessly versatile synthetic was the material of choice for postwar designers. It could be molded, fused, laminated, and colored any hue in the rainbow. Natural wood, glass, and ceramics were often designed to imitate plastic shapes and finishes.

Check out ads in magazines from the era you're most interested in, since retro design

moves and changes throughout the decades. If you look through a 1953 issue of *Life*, for example, you might be inspired to design your home's living room to resemble a midcentury lounge. Stay stylistically faithful to the magazine's publication date by using furnishings in Formica, chrome, and plastic. Borrow greens, grays, and turquoise in muted tones for your upholstery. Accessories should be functional, yet true to the period. For 1953, this includes Bakelite ashtrays, art glass vases, and synthetic knit throws.

If you're looking for a style that manages to pull off the neat trick of looking historic, modern, and futuristic at the same time, think retro. Because in the retro universe, everything old is new again.

CLOCKWISE FROM ABOVE LEFT: Often inspired by architecture, Miuccia Prada's Miu Miu line recalls the 1970s honeycomb architecture of the New Otani hotel in Paris but is softened with rounded edges and a classic-seventies burnt-yellow and rust color palette. Stripes of all shapes and sizes as well as plastic accessories can wink at the past while still remaining fresh for today.

floral
m All Star
For details,
g Guide.

# resort

TRADE YOUR BRIEFCASE FOR A BEACH TOTE, spend your days searching for shells, and drift off to sleep in your private beachside bungalow. Break out your Polynesian-patterned shirts and Brigitte Bardot bikinis, and push inhibitions aside. Adopt an unflappable "don't worry, be happy" attitude. This is what resort style is all about.

A legacy of the golden age of ocean travel, cruise-wear collections (popularly called resort wear) give serious designers a chance to cut loose and lighten up. Dressed in cosmopolitan casuals, the rich and famous can unwind in style. Emilio Pucci's beachwear basks in sun-bleached pastels. Missoni's loose-fitting cover-ups make sunset cruises more colorful. And Tory Burch's playful tunics and halter dresses shout "summer fun."

The resort color palette frequently goes beachcombing for its inspirations. Warm neutrals reflect sand, driftwood, and sea grass, and rosy tints surface from coral reefs. If you prefer greens and blues, a handful of sea glass is all you need to find an appealing analogous color theme.

Resort color combinations influenced by Carmen Miranda feature a mélange of tropical fruit tones or exotic floral hues. For a bright look, give turquoise, papaya orange, and lime green a try. Stir in a hint of lemon yellow or tangerine.

Resort patterns easily navigate between the shoals of sophistication and the whirlpool of silliness. Women in Lilly Pulitzer's Palm Beach paisley shifts parade hand in hand along the sand with men in cabana-stripe jammers. Whether you prefer bright solids or perky prints, it's fun to use your fashion favorites in your home's decor.

For your home's summer wardrobe, use lighthearted designs printed on breathable cotton on duvets, chair slipcovers, and pillows. On the porch and patio and poolside, water- and fade-resistant fabrics are a great choice. Make a visual pun on a paper parasol in a piña colada by using one of Missoni's splashy prints to cover a French market-sized umbrella poolside.

Natural linens, frequently used by fashion designers for summer wear, are perfect for sofas. Ottomans and chairs can be upholstered to match, but lush jungle prints and leafy designs may also be used. Pebble-surfaced barkcloth in hibiscus, bougainvillea, and other botanical prints offers an authentic island feel, as does mosquito netting over an outdoor daybed.

Like any resort ensemble, your home's decor requires just the right accessories—such as travel memorabilia, journals, or an antique suitcase tucked into the corner. If your preferred view of the water is from a boat, add nautical motifs, maritime collectibles, or model boats. And if you'd rather watch surfers catch waves while you sit on the sand, use a retro longboard for an eye-catching table surface.

No matter where you live, create the illusion of Saint-Tropez sunshine by unfurling striped awnings outside your windows or adding plantation shutters inside. Keep your windows bare or minimally dressed with sheer panels.

Don't forget the effect a cooling ocean breeze can have on your mood. Nothing brings back that summer feeling like white curtains gently blowing in the breeze. A ceiling fan with woven-palm paddle blades is the next best thing to the wind itself. Little could possibly be better than a nap in an indoor hammock.

For those who spend their life—or just their weekends—in pink Bermuda shorts, straw hats, and Havaianas flip-flops, resort style makes every day a vacation.

OPPOSITE AND ABOVE, CLOCKWISE FROM ABOVE LEFT: Shells of all shapes and sizes, watery blues, exotic prints, hibiscus flowers, and floating graphics à la Emilio Pucci's timeless prints for this bikini can all bring a relaxed and tropical ambience to an interior design.

From le
Adler's
floor la
shade, A
Halling
chair; D
na's ace
and nyl
**Jil Sand**
shoe, M
felt bra
silk gaz
moiré d

# modern

MODERN STYLE LIVES LIFE ON THE EDGE. A little bit classic, a little bit pop culture, it re-invents itself along the way and pushes new possibilities forward.

Whether reading a book by the latest experimental novelist or sitting in an iconic Mies van der Rohe Barcelona chair, today's modernist looks to both the future and the past for inspirations. Modern style means embracing change and constantly striving to improve the world through good design and technology.

From Yves Saint Laurent's groundbreaking "Mondrian" day dress of color-blocked wool jersey to Martin Margiela's clever ways with new edges, visible hems, linings, and seams—modernists like to turn the world inside out.

The modern-style home is a universe defined in black and white. Its yin and yang approach relies on dramatic contrasts for impact. Small strokes of intense hues, often red or yellow, add unexpected jolts of excitement. If using only black and white in a room is too strong a statement for you, go softer with tones

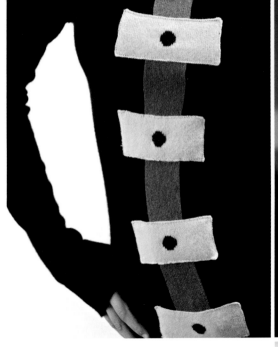

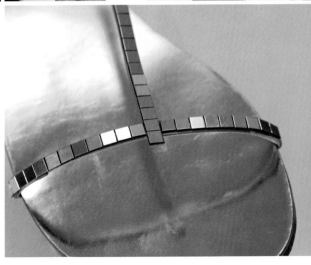

CLOCKWISE FROM ABOVE LEFT: Graphic and bold, with minimal color but maximum impact, is a modernist's design strategy in this appliquéd sweater, Amaya Arzuaga's graphic dress, Badgley Mischka's patent-leather handbag, and these Paco Rabanne–inspired mirrored sandals.

of gray and white. By blending charcoal and deep shades of brown, as modernist designer Andre Putman did for the New York Morgans Hotel, you will still have a graphic look, but warmer.

Working with a limited palette of any two colors located opposite each other on the color wheel is another option. High-octane blue with orange or bold purple with yellow are perfect examples. In a modern-style home, the proportions of dark versus light are what create atmosphere. Lean heavily toward lightness and your room will be quiet and airy. Go darker and the look feels moody and loungelike.

While the colors for your furniture, curtains, tableware, and decorative pieces are largely a foregone conclusion, mixing patterns provides endless options for creativity. Some modern textile designers reinterpret the past with a slightly skewed sense of humor. Instead of abandoning traditional motifs, they simply enlarge them. Checks become monumental; leafy motifs are blown up to giant proportions and cropped into abstraction. Modern patterns frequently demonstrate "back to nature" values.

"The key to understanding modern style is viewing both fashion and interior design as art."

Florence Broadhurst's wallpaper patterns feature egrets, horses, and large-scale flamboyant leaflike patterns along with neoclassic geometrics. It may seem ironic that Broadhurst's designs are still considered avant-garde, but this illustrates that many modern designs look as innovative today as when they were originally created. This means you won't necessarily need to pay premium prices to decorate your home using goods sold at tragically hip home furnishings shops. Cast-aluminum tulip tables by Eero Saarinen and innovative lighting by Dutch designer Marcel Wanders can often be found at vintage warehouses and flea markets.

Like a simple Marni dress enlivened with patent leather boots, and a few plastic bangle bracelets, decorative accessories make the modern home come alive in a subtle way. Add outrageous trimming onto solid white curtains. Toss abstract pillows onto a black leather sofa. Mimic shiny patent leather with high-gloss paint for a lacquerlike finish.

White is the modern home's equivalent of basic black. A room decorated entirely with solid white furniture can be accented with two-toned rugs, patterned pillows, and randomly layered draperies. Modular furniture, especially sectional sofas and tables sold in jigsaw-puzzle-like units, can be purchased in two contrasting tones and is perfect for modern, family-friendly rooms and awkward spaces.

The key to understanding modern style is viewing both fashion and interior design as art. Draperies that close with jumbo zippers or oversized buttons echo the bizarre coats and cloaks of André Courrèges. Metallic cube tables mirror Paco Rabanne's dresses made of aluminum plates and brass wire. To this end, home furnishings should be given sufficient space in order to be fully appreciated. Let an edgy graphic poster or an asymmetrical sofa you've selected speak for itself. If you're in doubt about anything—a color, a texture, a shape—leave it out. Like Philip Johnson's minimalist glass boxes, modern style is as transparent as a crystal ball. But first, you must master the art of looking into the future.

# eclectic

ECLECTIC STYLE HAS BOUNDLESS POTENTIAL for invention and makes anything possible. Constantly evolving, it is best defined by what it is not. Never exclusive or rigid, eclectic style doesn't live by the rules. When asked to make a choice, a true eclectic usually opts for "miscellaneous."

Adopt an eclectic vocabulary and you eliminate the "match" in "mix and match." It's a spectacular panorama of old and new, formal and funky. Drawing inspiration from different styles, periods, and places, eclectic style creates a one-of-a-kind collage from perennial favorites, new passions, and passing fancies. It's the sum of everything you love.

Sometimes subversive, sometimes sweet, eclectic looks are always intriguing. It takes guts to pair a flouncy chiffon dress with Old West cowboy boots instead of ballet flats, but Christian Lacroix knows his loyal devotees often dance to a different drummer. Marni, the successful Italian label designed by Consuela Castiglioni, concocts outfits in offbeat colors and textural combinations for her open-minded

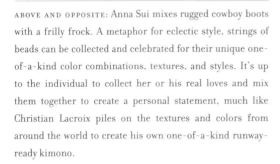

ABOVE AND OPPOSITE: Anna Sui mixes rugged cowboy boots with a frilly frock. A metaphor for eclectic style, strings of beads can be collected and celebrated for their unique one-of-a-kind color combinations, textures, and styles. It's up to the individual to collect her or his real loves and mix them together to create a personal statement, much like Christian Lacroix piles on the textures and colors from around the world to create his own one-of-a-kind runway-ready kimono.

audience, while Vivienne Westwood's bold and daring mixes of high-society sophistication and punk-rock glamour are sure to thrill a true eclectic aficionado.

Eclectic style's common denominator is a uniquely personal perspective. You can devise a color palette using the colors of a sunset and then add a few neon hues, or distill the rich essence of the seventeenth century, then embellish with modern pastels. You also may want to choose one color or color family to act as the "continuous thread" and create a harmonious decor that is still eclectic.

Monochromatic schemes with light, medium, and dark shades of the same color work especially well together. No matter what styles, eras, or design modes you combine, a room whose major pieces are painted or upholstered in

shades of blue and accessorized with blue, aqua, and pale green touches will be utterly blissful.

For those who don't want to limit their color choices, an all-white wall scheme is another option. Paint your home's walls in pure or tinted white and let each piece of furniture and decorative object stand out against the neutral background.

On the other hand, displaying items from your wilder days may lead you to choose op-art or paisley-covered wallpaper. Or if paying homage to the beach where you met your soul mate inspires a vibrant turquoise and coral color scheme, that's fine, too. What is important is your connection to what you choose. In an eclectic home, not only do the colors have meaning, but the furnishings and accents also reveal a distinctive point of view.

The rooms in an eclectic home can resemble a series of unrelated short stories or be conceived as a continuous tale, illustrating a few important themes. Take an anecdotal approach and one room might recall a desert nomadic dwelling, another the Rock and Roll Hall of Fame, and a third a casual Tahitian spa. In a home with epic aspirations, however, each room is a splashy potpourri. You might mix signature colors from several styles, and show off a Buddha given to you by one of your old roommates, furniture from your childhood home, and a collection of cutting-edge contemporary art glass, all mixed together in one room-wide tableau. Family keepsakes might be encased in a curio cabinet while the blown-glass pieces sit on a coffee table.

In the same way that people who dress eclectically don't frequently wear outfits that look alike, homes decorated eclectically don't often resemble one another.

The freedom to combine a rustic pine table with a candy-colored Venetian glass chandelier is what makes an eclectic house user-friendly and fun. If you're a little shy about putting your personal passions and quirks on display for the world to see, you can start small. Hang one truly eccentric object or combine a few odd items into a tabletop conversation piece. Break a decorating rule or smash a decorating cliché. Give yourself license to do something different. After all, being eclectic is the most iconoclastic thing you can do in a world in which following fashion matters.

Making

per...
right...
and c...

...get under the covers, close
...off to sleep. Here's how to select
...and sheets to help you create that
...environment you've been dreaming of.

DUCED BY REBECCA THIENES  WRITTEN BY ELIZABETH ROEHRIG

# vintage

NOT AT ALL OLD-FASHIONED, VINTAGE STYLE is a contemporary celebration of frosted cupcakes, flowery print dresses, and the simple joy of living.

Nostalgic in a lighthearted way, vintage style conveys an ideal version of the past, when the world was a simpler place. Ralph Lauren designs slinky halter dresses Jean Harlow would have loved, Betsey Johnson brightens innocent prom dresses with shots of color and tulle, and Oscar de la Renta recalls ballerinas of the 1920s and '30s with his feather-and-tulle confections.

Whether they're found in fashion or home decor, vintage style's gently faded blues, pinks, greens, and lilacs are muted without feeling dreary. Colors with a floral inspiration—periwinkle blue, rose pink, buttercup yellow—can easily be mixed into a heady bouquet. A palette of soft and yellow-infused whites looks as fresh as a summer's day. Silver accents add sparkling touches to the details of your room.

Although inspired by the past, today's vintage color palette doesn't always mimic a specific era. It evokes a feeling rather than an authentic look. Pair a teal tone borrowed from a French Provençal porcelain clock with a simple British colonial cream, or juxtapose a trio of pinks from wherever and whenever.

Like a classic Roger Vivier clutch, vintage rooms have the kind of beauty and character that comes only with age. Faintly rumpled sateen sheets, slightly sun-bleached curtains, and much-laundered linens are irresistible throwbacks. Previously owned rhinestone buckles, silver vanity sets, and curio boxes offer reminders of a glamorous past.

A bookcase with peeling paint, china crackled with tiny lines, and a brass bed frame rich with patina add personality to a home. Just as a vintage evening skirt inspires daydreams of a moonlit terrace and Mr. Right, a set of green jadeite dishes conjures up an image of sitting down to a farmhouse breakfast at an enamel kitchen table with crisp white curtains blowing in the breeze.

Whether they are family heirlooms or flea-market finds, items that have been cherished and passed on for generations look fabulous, especially when combined in imaginative ways. Display quirky bric-a-brac in an eccentric container, or create a patchwork of tarnished silver and clothbound books on wall shelves. Pile random sun-faded print cushions on an assortment of interesting old chairs on your porch. Hang a gallery of secondhand oil paintings in your living room. Create a kitchen border with

salvaged embossed tiles. Make entertaining a blast with vintage barware and serving pieces mixed with colorful contemporary china. Repurpose treasures that no longer need to serve their original intention.

Decor inspired by the past often must make concessions to present times. Instead of outfitting your kitchen with restored appliances from the 1930s and '40s, try updated versions with modern features and vintage style. Many appliances are available in the pastel shades of pink, turquoise, and mint popular fifty and sixty years ago. Soak modern candy-stripe cotton or floral linen fabrics in a tea bath to achieve an aged look, as if they were genuine antiques.

In today's fast-moving world, the concept of coming home to a soothing vintage decor and leaving the modern world behind is enormously appealing. In the vintage-style home, the charm of nostalgia permeates—and perks up—day-to-day life.

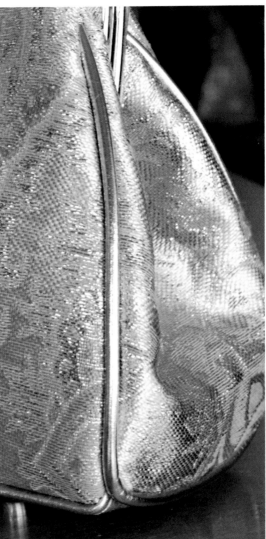

OPPOSITE AND ABOVE: Vintage details, such as the rhinestone guppy swallowing a huge aquamarine on this sandal or the pale pink fur shrug to warm the shoulders, add a subtle sense of humor along with old-world charm. Lighter shades of blue and silver from Oscar de la Renta keep the weight of the past in check.

BOUQUET
CHAMPÊTRE

16:29

## eco

ECO IS ALL ABOUT REUSING, RECYCLING, and renewing. Going green means living lightly off the land, eating organically grown foods, and doing the right thing for the world community. In tune with nature, simple by design, and sensible for the planet, this environmentally and socially sensitive style is essential for global living.

If you think all eco fashions are designed for the Birkenstock crowd, however, think again. Today's "green" fashionista has plenty of options that are not only pleasing to the eye but require no sacrifice in comfort or design. Linda Loudermilk's eco-luxury fashions are edgy yet earth-friendly in mud-dyed linen, milk cashmere, and seaweed silks. Enamore, a creative British fashion house, produces flirty lingerie and fifties-style frocks using organic soya and sustainable hemp fabrics, along with recycled materials. Rogan Gregory's casual skirts, jeans, tops, and hoodies for Loomstate Organic are stitched from organic cotton grown without synthetic fertilizer or chemicals. Rock superstar

Bono and wife Ali Hewson's EDUN label brings high style to slacks, chiffon dresses, and short-cropped blazers while promoting social justice and sustainable development in the poorest African nations.

Eco colors celebrate Mother Nature's diversity through vibrant greens, earthy neutral tones, and sunset hues. Admirers of eco style are frequently concerned with the source of the color pigments used to tint fibers and fabrics. Instead of the usual chemically dyed rainbow of choices, eco cottons come in unbleached whites and color-grown shades of blue, green, brown, and purple. Sheep and alpaca wools produce a range of soft, lovely undyed colors, too. Colors derived from berries, vegetables, minerals, and earth irons extend the range even further. Blacks are obtained from coal, soot, or charcoal; shades of red come from various types of clay.

Just as New York artist and designer Susan Cianciolo fuses a sense of fashion with earth-friendly materials, ecologically minded home furnishing designers feature rattan and wicker or hardwoods like ebony, teak, cocobolo, or rosewood harvested from sustainable sources. Bamboo is one of nature's most renewable resources and can be used to manufacture window shades, wood-like flooring, rugs, and upholstery fabrics. Abaca hemp accessories and wall-to-wall sisal floor mats enhance the natural look of any space.

In an eco kitchen, walls are painted with soy or milk paints colored with mineral pigments, butcher-block counters are made from sustain-

"Eco colors celebrate Mother Nature's diversity through vibrant greens, earthy neutral tones, and sunset hues."

able wood, and dish towels are woven from organic cotton produced without using chemicals. Bedroom furniture is all recycled vintage pieces; mattresses are made of latex gathered from rubber trees by workers who receive a fair share of the profits; and bed linens are stitched from organic cotton, washed in only baking soda and vegetable soap. Respect for the earth, a desire to live healthier, and support for non-exploitive business practices are all factored into the decorating process.

Inspired by majestic mountains, bottomless oceans, and brilliantly colored flora and fauna, eco patterns allow the human body and spirit to reaffirm its deep connection to the natural world. Even if the rest of your home is filled with solid-color furnishings, your children's rooms can become oases of ecological motifs, such as a rain forest–inspired mural.

Want to preserve more of nature and provide a healthier future for the next generation? Reducing the amount of new items you buy is the surest way to accomplish that. Like Stella McCartney's fashions, made with recycled fabrics and trims, a home built with salvaged architectural materials and decorated with flea-market table linens and recycled home goods like glassware made from returned soda bottles is a great start.

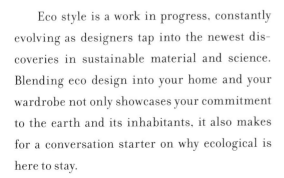

Eco style is a work in progress, constantly evolving as designers tap into the newest discoveries in sustainable material and science. Blending eco design into your home and your wardrobe not only showcases your commitment to the earth and its inhabitants, it also makes for a conversation starter on why ecological is here to stay.

COUNTERCLOCKWISE FROM ABOVE RIGHT: Mother Nature inspires this frock of fronds, while designer Susan Cianiolo shows us that eco and edgy can go hand in hand. Unadorned, unpolished stones show the raw beauty of quartzite color, which can easily translate into both an earthy and ephemeral color palette for a washroom.

# mixing fashionable home decor

THE FUN OF DECORATING COMES FROM COMBINING YOUR STYLE CHOICES (AND THOSE OF YOUR FAMILY MEMBERS) IN YOUR LIVING SPACE. IT'S THE COMBINATION OF THESE DIFFERENT FASHION STYLES THAT MAKES YOUR HOME A UNIQUE EXPRESSION OF YOU.

And just as your favorite fashions change throughout your life, the fashion styles you choose for your home can also evolve and be woven together as well. For example, while the basics of your wardrobe have probably stayed the same over the years, you may have become more courageous in your color choices or added some bohemian accessories inspired by your travels. Or you may have changed in your taste for bohemian styles and returned to the comfort of classic khakis and crisp button-downs. Infusing your personal style into your home decor will make you feel at home in your space.

The following twenty rooms will show you in both a broad sense and a more detailed sense how master mixers have translated the runway to the room in their own homes. As you peruse the pictures, you'll probably find touches of a few more styles than the two main influences named. Think of the essence of what you want your room to say, or your two favorite styles as seen in the design style guide (page 35), and then throw in your own elements of surprise to keep your rooms looking fresh. For example, in my couture bohemian dining room, you'll see that all of the collected old elements have an eclectic and vintage vibe.

As you embark on your own decorating journey, the inspiration boards that show the fashion influences behind each room mix should prompt you to dig deep in your closet to find your own layered style to put into practice in your rooms. Your everyday wardrobe and its colors and textures will give you a hint of what kind of fabrics you want to use in high-traffic rooms. Studying your accessories—vintage rhinestone earrings, funky platform clogs, or color-charged modern plastic bangles from the 1950s—may give you an idea of how you'd like to accessorize your basics pieces. Here, in the accessories department, because the commitment isn't as big or as costly as with major pieces of furniture, is where I encourage you to experiment with mixing and layering.

# |COUTURE BOHEMIAN| royal charm

IN MY DINING ROOM, I CHOSE MY DREAMS of faraway places, my love of a fresh garden palette, and my fondness for handmade custom details to be the two main style inspirations: bohemian and couture. Over the years my style and choices for this room have changed and grown as my life becomes more full, and at times, more complex. Given my ever-growing and -changing life, I decided to go with a bohemian style that embraces the idea of adding and evolving. With four children, the idea of actually sitting down to a civilized dinner can be a dream. But just the same, I continue to hold on to hope that as we all get older (the kids, too) sophisticated dinner parties will transform from dream to reality. That more dressed-up dream plays into the couture influence found in my dining room.

I'm the first to admit that as a family of six, we're just not that fancy. But there's a side of me that loves the idea of a formal dinner, like the one we enjoy each year as a family for Valentine's Day. These "dress-up" moments, however infrequent, are the couture side of me coming out to play.

BY JEFFREY WESTBROOK

couture bohemian

158

Anything can happen around the central square table surrounded by mix-and-match chairs—two gold and pink Louis XV ones that are more than seventy-five years old, and a mix of Chinese lacquered ones—that reflect my love for bringing different eras and styles together. Setting a table with an adventurous tone is another way to show a bohemian side. Here, gold place mats from a friend's visit to India and brocade runners reflect a couture-inspired "gold standard," as luxuriant as Versace bangles and Moroccan glasses etched with gold sparkle. Christian Lacroix, the iconic king of high-octane color mixed in a couture bohemian way, could easily have provided the inspiration behind the bohemian blend of my colorful collected china. Each table setting offers couture and bohemian styles, with intricately embroidered napkins set with mismatched silverware. At the table's center, fresh celadon hydrangeas soak in an antique silver wine bucket—a simple touch that makes a big visual impact, like an oversized vintage pin on a plain brown coat.

Asian elements—Chinese and Indian artwork—have been layered around the room and against the large framed-out panels on the walls of the dining room. I chose to put chinoiserie wallpaper on these characteristically craftsman panels to create a story in the room and add the fresh shade of a golden green, almost like adding a decorating "garnish" to our meals. The touches of gold and pink in the dining room wallpaper blend nicely into the adjacent living room, keeping a harmonious flow with a touch of formality. The delicate and floating flora and fauna of the wallpaper add a sense of whimsy while providing contrast to the heavier dining room chairs. For the room's elegant silk curtains, which uphold the room's formality, I was inspired by Kate and Laura Mulleavy of Rodarte, two forward-thinking fashion designers whose innovative mixes with meticulous attention to detail are simple yet dramatic.

The grounding force in the room is the antique sideboard. It's a heavy old piece that I found at one of my favorite antique stores. I store my collection of china and silver inside. On top, I've layered an old mirror with a couple of Indian prints that were gifts from friends. A couture-inspired decorative silver five-arm candelabrum with simple white tapers also sits at the ready on the sideboard, to be easily moved to the table for more bohemian-styled illumination.

Additional light, critical to the success of any room, comes in the form of the amber blown-glass ceiling fixture hanging just above the large square table. Reminiscent of a Moroccan hanging lamp found at a bazaar, it adds a nice, warm Eastern glow to the room.

The Asian garden–like wallpaper creates a relaxing place to dine while providing a subtle and exotic backdrop to the bohemian mix of French, Indian, and Moroccan artwork and tableware.

With its bohemian accents and its couture detailing on the accessories and furnishings, my dining room is just as ready for champagne at cocktail hour as it is for mint tea in the afternoon. I love this room because, as with my wardrobe, I can always add more color, more textures, and more alluring details, which are the essence of both couture and bohemian style.

ABOVE AND OPPOSITE: Amber and gold offer a regal palette in this couture bracelet. Table napkins, place mats, and cutlery offer a jewel box of details to the setting. A kaleidoscope of color often used by Alexander McQueen in his couture collections mixes the bohemian globe-trotting aesthetic with the sparkle of couture details as found in this Indian print and gold-leafed tea glasses displayed on my dining room buffet.

## |VINTAGE CASUAL| homecoming queen

THERE'S NOTHING LIKE THE WARMTH AND strength of an object that bucks all trends and stands the test of time. Whether it's a beat-up old denim jacket or a pistachio-colored collection of jadeite bowls from the thirties, there's something comforting about reaching for an item that's tried and true. Such is the case in Mary's vintage and casual kitchen. Filled with collections of mint-julep- and white-colored bits and pieces—from old California pottery to 1940s small appliances and pale-green-colored juice glasses picked up at local flea markets—her Southern California bungalow kitchen is a study in blending the charm of yesteryear with the demands of today.

As you enter through oversized double Dutch doors, the mood is instantly warm and welcoming. By removing the wall between the cooking and eating areas, Mary created an open and friendly atmosphere where kids and neighbors can casually gather to watch what's cooking without worrying about leaving a mark on the already-weathered oak floors or charmingly chipped original cabinets. In fact, in keeping with the family's child-friendly life, the owners kept the original oak flooring, knowing that scuffs would serve to enrich its character, not detract from it. Similarly, a large weathered old kitchen table begs for visitors to sit and stay awhile, while serving as the center for an ever-evolving collection of chairs that Mary picks up and changes around. While the look may have a feminine vintage flair in pale shades of cream and green, it's the patina and openness of the room that make it feel down-home and casual.

Study her collections: jadeite—that milky-green glassware built, like denim, to be stain-resistant and used every day; Fire King plates; Anchor Hocking glassware; old crystal cabinet pulls. All may appear to be girlie on their sparkling surfaces, but underneath, they're tough as nails.

Mary's color choices, too, evoke both softness and strength. A classic creamy white offers a calming base as it's painted on both the original Shaker-style cabinets and plank-wood walls, in addition to the open shelves, which hold her ever-growing and -changing collections of glassware, teapots, and servers. Lighthearted

vintage casual

pastels of green and blue and a few rosy-pink accents have that same vintage yet casual appeal of a Nanette Lepore summer dress. Schoolhouse fixtures, a butcher-block countertop, and an old apron sink offer the hardworking balance to the soft palette, much like a pair of boots can take the froufrou out of a floral frock.

Fabrics, too, work hard while not loosing their femininity. Framing the kitchen window in mismatched lace and tulle lets in the light while not looking too precious, just as Vivienne Westwood would mix tulle and lace in a casual way. Old-denim blue and ticking stripes mix and match as cushions, handmade out of remnants too small for a couch but perfect to soften an old chair.

Much like tweaking an old family recipe for the needs of today, Mary has added just enough down-home quirks to her kitchen full of flea-market finds to keep it hardworking, organized, and ready to roll for the next welcome visitor.

Mary's kitchen is a study of the "so what?" Southern California vintage casual aesthetic . . . the more scuffs, company, collections, flowers, and sunshine, the better. This relaxed atmosphere of organized clutter with a dash of ingenuity (check out the mirror over the kitchen sink to mimic a window or to see who's coming) is the hallmark of a great kitchen.

OPPOSITE AND RIGHT: Mary maximizes the sunlight pouring in through her window by displaying her collections of light-catching glass, pearly buttons, and a vintage dog-show trophy on the sill while a mix-and-match assortment of glassware lines the kitchen shelves. The floral flare makes these vintage party shoes a favorite. The influence of this Betsey Johnson frock shows that vintage can mean fun and humor.

## |RETRO MODERN| smooth transition

SOPHISTICATED LOUNGE LIVING—KICKED UP with acidic brights and Paul Smith–inspired stripes—comes alive in this retro modern home. Bold graphics, eye-popping color, and a spotlight on play are just the ticket for a single dad of two. A New York native, the owner shed every ounce of his former East Coast conservatism in favor of a more relaxed California style.

Because he shares his bachelor space with his two kids on the weekends, masculine elements had to be balanced with energetic fun. Case in point: the color palette. Serious browns and rich muted teals on the walls and floors are given a lift with hits of citrus in key accessories and simple bicolor art.

Centered with a curvy olive-shaded rug patterned after ocean rocks, the rug gives fluid movement to a room largely filled with angles and lines. The amoeba-shaped Noguchi coffee table also balances the room's angles. Since this modern classic was first introduced in 1948, the polished curvilinear shape has added functional

retro modern

side tables for the kids' grazing buffet, and a fiery orange quilted throw. "Urban" chairs, $40 each, and "Lack" side tables, $13 each, ikea .com for stores. Blanket, $125, urbanoutfitters.com.

grace to any room of any era. Hugging the ebony and tinted-glass table, an L-shaped sectional sofa in comfy and durable mossy-green microfiber chenille offers versatility. The kids' favorite for movie night, the sofa is as streamlined and comfortable as an old pair of Tod's driving shoes. It can stand alone unadorned, or in this case, take a warm turn when plumped with orange, fig, and white hand-screened pillows.

Two bright orange cylindrical mini beanbags serve double duty as footstool poufs and lounge seating for kids. A matching orange foam rocker sits at ground level next to a floor lamp in high-gloss white for catching up on homework or reading. Dressed in white canvas cotton with large grommets for easy gliding, the curtains frame the window, and rattan Roman shades offer more privacy and a touch of earthiness to the sixties- and seventies-retro modern pad. Like good ol' Jack Purcell original Converse tennies with extra hefty grommets in fresh white canvas, these touches offer fresh appeal to the teal- and brown-hued loftlike space.

Although the living room is wide open for an array of activities, a bump-out on the white-curtained window wall offers the perfect spot

FOLLOWING PAGES: An upbeat palette of retro mixed with the modernity of an open loft give this dad and his kids a no-fuss living space in which all surfaces are both comfortable and cleanable.

for Dad's home office. Sitting underneath an aqua-hued David Hockney painting is a grass green Philippe Starck chair for Kartell, where the home owner can quietly work amid the exuberant and open space.

Segmented off by a deep-fig shade of paint, the dining area features a shiny contemporary Italian walnut-wood table, a study in functionality and minimalism that lets meals take center stage. Punctuating the table's quiet demeanor are the Omar de Biaggio B-Pop Side Chairs, whose SKU-style colorful stripes bring to mind a classic and eye-popping Harvie & Hudson dress shirt. Dizzying stripes on dining chairs of periwinkle, tangerine, chartreuse, and sky blue are the pièce de résistance of this retro modern family space.

Just as quirky stripes can take the sting out of putting on a dress shirt for work, so can a few shots of color liven up a home and uplift this working dad's loft—like a masculine retreat.

OPPOSITE: A mix of high and low style fills this working dad's home-office niche, including a David Hockney original sitting above his desk, which holds simple Ikea plastic boxes in just the right shade of blue.

ABOVE RIGHT: A throw pillow of vivid orange and cream in a graphic chain-link pattern perks up the more sedate solid mossy green sofa and muted teal wall.

BELOW RIGHT: Paul Smith nails resort-bright knits with his punchy palette of kelly green, tangerine, and hot pink with the added shimmer and modernity of Lurex.

|ECO BOHEMIAN| conscientious
retreat

NESTLED IN THE URBAN NEIGHBORHOOD OF
Echo Park, near the heart of downtown Los
Angeles, an outdoor haven emerges. Honking
horns and busy bustle are replaced by a dreamy
setting in which nature is celebrated, a gypsylike
lifestyle thrives, and the days are whiled away in
this eco bohemian garden retreat.

In just two hundred square feet, a modern-
day fairy tale unfolds in this green space. With
its focus on nature and appreciation for all
things ethnic, the tiny backyard is a celebration
of both eco and the extraordinary. Picture the
fashion influence here as a combination of
organic denim Loomstate jeans, an organic
cotton Patagonia T, and an oversized hemp
satchel filled with the latest book on growing
organics in the garden. This backyard is pure
and playful; synthetics and plastics have been
banned from the party.

At the heart of this outdoor sanctuary rests a
bamboo canopy that lures prospective loungers,
complete with gauzy curtains on all four sides to

eco bohemian

ABOVE AND OPPOSITE: Mathew Williamson, a self-described magpie, loves to adorn his bohemian collections with a bit of shimmer and sparkle, much like this eco-bohemian outdoor lounge is adorned with exotic patterns and color.

protect one from pesky mosquitoes. Originally handmade by the owner for his beach wedding, the canopy has now been skillfully repurposed, using additional bamboo found at a local import store: as the saying goes, "Waste not, want not."

Recycling and repurposing is an inherent part of being green, from building to fashion. Eco-conscious designers like Susan Cianciolo work with recycled fabrics whenever possible, just as this home owner made—and then reused—his backyard bamboo canopy.

Bamboo, one of the world's most highly renewable plants, is also a textile of choice for many eco clothing designers like Kate O'Connor and eco-pioneering clothing companies like Patagonia. From canopy to bedsheets to breathable, beautiful apparel, bamboo fabrics are a great way to accentuate an eco-conscious room decor.

The exotic energy in this backyard says nomad, but everything else about it invites you in to stay for a while. White linen welcomes you to read, relax, and daydream in a tonal palette of woodsy browns, foliage greens, and pops of coral and rosy pink. Primitive patterned pillows on the canopied bed-cum-lounger enliven the white lounging spot with eye-popping hot pinks, reds, yellows, and greens taken from the garden. Collected from one trip to the next, these pillows—or at least the fabrics they are covered in—have traveled great distances to get to this backyard. Handmade by Uzbekistan artisans,

the embroidered suzani cushions provide a joyful explosion of handmade silk needlework in bold, graphic patterns. The multicolored Moroccan lamps bought at a local shop create yet another accent of bohemian living.

Outside the tented getaway rests a central seating area of tree-trunk furniture fashioned in a style similar to that of Brazilian furniture designer Hugo Franca. A visionary, this artisan sculpts furniture from fallen and burned pequi hardwood scavenged from the Amazon's coastal rain forest. From the simple table and chairs comes a conversation on the ecological importance of forest stewardship and the respect and reuse of both new and ancient wood. A hand-turned bowl is a wonderful example of American woodworking craftsmanship and a receptacle for nature's simple gifts, including the just-picked pomegranates that rest in its hub.

On the continuing journey of transferring the inside out, multiple ethnic rugs in white, beige, brown, and orange accents craft a comfortable sitting-room feeling in the great outdoors. All of the global influences, from the far-flung suzani pillows in hand-dyed saturated hues to the eco-inspired bamboo canopy, let this outside hideaway capture an ephemeral style that balances feel-good responsibility with feel-good relaxation.

OPPOSITE AND ABOVE: Burlwood from the 1970s is making an ecological return, here shown as an outdoor dining set, while a rainbow of bright pastel bangles and pattern-on-pattern mellow-yellow chiffon also recall the same easygoing and earth-friendly seventies era.

# |RESORT MODERN| island noir

UNDERNEATH THE WHITEWASHED PITCHED roof of this house, it's always vacation time. You can practically feel the clean, salty air circulating through the interiors, thanks to the resort-meets-modern-style decor embraced for this living room.

This interior designer's family of five wanted their living room to capture happy memories of summers spent in Mexico and Hawaii, but they preferred to balance the tropical style with a modish simplicity to keep the household with three kids calm and cool. This is reflected in the black and white modern-style backdrop the designer and home owner chose for the living room. A fresh wash of bright white paint covers the wood-beamed ceiling, walls, and even fireplace mantel, while black accents the framed wall art and covers the family's corduroy sofa. There is also a 1950s black-lacquer bamboo coffee table.

With the high-contrast palette in place for the backdrop of the room, the palm green, bright turquoise, and papaya yellow accent colors pop like a chunky stone necklace pops against a black and white Diane von Furstenberg wrap dress. A large-scale palm-frond print of easy-care linen dresses the chaise lounge and the toss cushion on the black svelte sofa. An easy hand-screened aloha print of khaki and saturated turquoise covers two neatly squared and piped floor cushions.

Another calm and cool element this room offers is the serenity of symmetry. Balancing (both in color and in form) the linear black sofa are two matching Asian-inspired curled-leg side tables in glossy white laminate that sit on either side. Resting on the pair of flanking tables are two tall and curvaceous matching lamps that pay a white monochromatic homage to modernity, circa the sixties, much like André Courrèges, one of the inventors of the "mod" style, used glossy white fabrics for his simple minis.

Accessories, too, give this spare room some tropical punch, with quirky Hawaiiana in the form of old parrot and Polynesian girl ceramics filled with easy-to-care-for simple tropical foliage and flowers. The wall art has more contemporary graphic appeal, with the main piece above the sofa of a teal and acid-green butterfly wing and another with a big black and white parrot humorously gazing at the viewer.

While resort wear gives fashion designers the opportunity to cut loose for a midwinter collection, a commitment to the personal design

resort modern

ethos they've worked so hard to establish always remains within sight. Similarly, this space maintains the interior designer's grown-up love of modernity, while still entertaining the memories of being a child on summer break. It's Hampton style with an aloha attitude, just like an Emilio Pucci print is as much about modernity as it is about play.

Despite the home's three kids and a jam-packed life, all the colorful yet restrained design elements of this room offer a nice balance of uncluttered minimalism with the playfulness of paradise.

OPPOSITE: A 1940s sunny yellow settee boasts a band of brass tacks that echoes the leaf pattern in the chaise, and the brass in the swooping floor lamp above.

ABOVE LEFT: The home owner's wardrobe of red Capri heels, acid-yellow clutch, and gauzy green and white blouse provided the easy inspiration for the family's tropical living room.

ABOVE RIGHT: Piles of colorful books, old Hawaiian ceramics, and a few fresh flowers keep the modern space happy and lively.

# |CLASSIC CASUAL| man of the house

MARRYING THE STATELY NATURE OF A LIBRARY with heartfelt hospitality isn't easy, but it's mission accomplished with this rich and tweedy room. Here, classic library appointments—books, globes, maps—seamlessly blend with a casual masculine style. Golds, browns, and burnished bronze colors mix nicely with dark woods and plush textures to create a comfortable atmosphere for reading, relaxing, or catching up on work.

Like Hemingway's Africa or the classic casual chic of a Burberry trench, the rich earth hues reflected in this library have limitless appeal. Custom walnut wall paneling with antique glazing wraps the room in a whiskey-shaded warmth, with an attention to cornices and moldings equal to the craftsmanship of an original Louis Vuitton steamer trunk. A generously proportioned English Bridgewater-style chair and ottoman encourage relaxation and contemplation, while a large and comfortable upholstered leather sofa encourages conversation in this British gentleman's clublike library.

classic casual

2

The walls of the library are filled with custom floor-to-ceiling built-in bookshelves that display antique books, many printed before 1800, as well as early-edition books that the owner's wife delights in discovering at garage sales. Old globes, large and small, of tin, cast iron, and cardboard, are clustered for display and study on the double-tiered coffee table, which also holds a revolving exhibit of large-scale illustrated books.

The lighting in the room invites reading in every corner, day or night. Hanging quietly above is a burnished bronze chandelier crowning the room in a simple, unadorned style, while small gilt wall sconces with contrasting cream shades illuminate the dark walnut walls. A few well-placed table lamps, including a nice period French brass lamp with a custom-made black-lacquered shade, provide a classic touch with easy use. Daytime study is equally easy, with plenty of natural light pouring through the classic floor-to-ceiling mullioned windows, reminiscent of an Ivy League library. With casual flaxen-hued drapes hung from no-fuss metal rod and rings, daylight is controlled by

FOLLOWING PAGES: The grand scale of this gentleman's library is made to feel homey and cozy with the use of a warm color palette of browns and ambers, and classic textures such as the herringbone-patterned wood floor and faux-croc drinks table.

"This pairing of 'important' with the unknown is another example of the room's casual mix with classic design."

a simple swish of a wand. In these easy window treatments, the casual-meets-classic style is apparent.

Just as a book can transport the reader to exotic locales, accessories in this room do the same. Along with the collections of globes and books, a large black-and-white photograph by renowned photographer Peter Beard entitled "Catching Rhinos in the Hunting Area" offers the room and the viewer a visual escape to Africa. Next to it, in another nod to the classic but casual British colonial style invoked in this room, sits a more casual reference to travel in the form of a primitive sculpture by an unknown artist. This pairing of "important" with the unknown is another example of the room's casual mix with classic design.

Just as an Yves Saint Laurent suit celebrates the masculine timeless and the wearable, with exotic touches to boot, so does this library serve up the studied sophistication of classic and warm design, while lending relaxed yet fascinating overtones. Taking cues from both classic and casual, this library will endure as long as the books that grace it.

OPPOSITE, ABOVE: African artifacts attract viewers with their primitive pull. The simple sculpture of a woman with her baby offsets the more masculine Beard black-and-white photograph of a charging rhino.

OPPOSITE, BELOW: In a sort of nouveau safari way, Tommy Hilfiger shows how to combine casual and classic in this vest and shirt combination tied together with shades of khaki, cream, and orange.

ABOVE LEFT: Plain flax linen French-pleated drapes get classic accents for interest: a border of a Greek key motif and burnished brass rod and rings.

ABOVE RIGHT: A collection of old globes both large and small pleases the home owner's travel-inspired aesthetic.

## |ECLECTIC MODERN| earthy elegance

WHO SAYS CONTEMPORARY HAS TO BE COLD? In this photographer's eclectic and modern apartment, the dining room resonates with chic sophistication and earthy warmth, thanks to a delicious chocolate and amber color palette outlined with crisp white trim and an array of well-edited and worldly accessories.

Traveling around the globe for her work, Karyn relishes every moment of her at-home time, a respite during which she surrounds herself with the things she loves and mementos from her far-flung travels. Case in point are Karyn's table and settings. All resting on her simple circular Eero Saarinen table, chic wooden place mats reminiscent of her recent safari in Africa hold classic English Staffordshire brown and white plates with heirloom linen napkins gifted by her favorite aunt, topped with treasured textiles found at another favorite source, in Antigua Guatemala. All the disparate objects work together beautifully because they've been handpicked by the home owner herself, and she has stylishly stuck to a simple natural color

eclectic modern

palette while playing up each item's texture. The warm and woodsy colors of the table and place mats are balanced with the luminescence of the pearly-white silverware and sparkly amber footed glasses. This combination lends a polished and feminine sparkle, much like a string of pearls or an old crystal brooch would add a touch of lightness and personality to a modern khaki ensemble.

The centerpiece, a single white circular melamine tray holding a trio of small succulents, makes a no-fuss, fresh statement without detracting from the rest of the dining room.

A modern take on eclecticism continues in the space's original whimsically-shaped white built-in corner shelves, which house Karyn's collection of 1920s era dishes and figurines. Because she chose to collect in white, all the antiques, including milk glass, porcelain puppy bookends, and sculpturally shaped teapots, are perfectly at home in a modern-style dining room, and keep the small space looking fresh against the deeper sepia walls. Just as a big white Birkin bag and some leopard-print slippers refresh a

Contrasting matte espresso-brown walls with pristine white trim frame this photographer's dining room, while warm midtoned woods in the Eero Saarinen tabletop, beaded place mats, and old oak floors round out the natural palette. Attention to symmetry and scale in the generously sized pendant lamp and table and chairs lend a comfortable, settled feeling to the dining area.

wardrobe of browns and beige, so do white wood-work and a few quirky accessories enliven a rich-toned room.

Continuing with the white accents, the glossy lacquered Chinese Chippendale–style chairs are softened with espresso- and honey-hued op-art polka-dot cushions. The rich color choice is both chic and wise, as the dark brown fabric easily disguises a few dinner-party mis-haps. Crowning the room is a cool nod to mod in the generously sized paper pendant lamp, which glows luminously over the table while adding yet another sculptural element to the room.

Plenty of natural light, too, pours in through a pair of artfully framed white windows with folds of luscious paisley curtains, bringing all the warm and natural tones of the room together. As the home owner is both an adventuress and an Anglophile at heart, the drapes also reflect her personal eclectic and modern style; she uses the paisley curtains much as she would use an Etro or Hermès paisley scarf, to tie an outfit together. Again, topped with clean white mold-ing, the bohemian paisley is reined in with the structure and simplicity of the curtain boxes.

A photographer has to constantly edit what appears through her lens, and this expert eye found the perfect balance of warmth and restraint in a room that imparts a comfortable yet lively ambience for sharing a meal or a cock-tail with friends.

OPPOSITE AND ABOVE: This photographer's apartment is a study of accessorizing with personality, as her heirloom ironstone plates, Guatemalan napkins, and even her leopard slippers doubling as décor. Diane von Furstenberg plays with an earthy elegance theme with a swingy crocheted suit matched with a graphic blouse—all in modern naturals.

## |ROMANTIC BOHEMIAN| la vie en rose

A MIX OF FARAWAY INFLUENCES, SOUVENIRS, and rose-hued accents makes this romantic bohemian boudoir an experience for the curious of mind. Like a journal filled with tales of a life well traveled, the room whisks you away from day-to-day reality and takes you to a luxurious resting place, where you are surrounded by mementos of worldly adventures.

In true bohemian style, the room swells with a mixture of jewel tones and exotic reminders of cultures, people, and places that its owner, Jane, has met along her travels. A Spanish shawl sits on the distressed wood of the desk chair. An array of embroidered flowers against shiny cream satin, the shawl calls to mind flamenco traditions and all things feminine and passionate. Furthering the room's unapologetic feminity, on top of the central bureau is an oil painting of a woman gazing out as if to survey the lush decor.

Like a sumptuous Claire Pettibone dressing gown, the textures and patterns in this bedroom

romantic bohemian

are as pleasing to the touch as to the eye, and the art of layering is in full bloom. The walls first attract the eye, covered in a light fabric that gracefully combines the exotic wildness of a leopard print with the European sensibility of a swirling paisley. A design motif with two thousand years of history to its credit, paisley adorns the hexagon-shaped Indian bedside table and dots the room with its familiar curve on pillows and blankets. Pink, the centerpiece of the room's color palette, fills the room with romance, from a soft-toned peony drape to the deep fuchsia in a striped pillow. Glittery, circular silver and gold Indian embroidery weaves throughout saris and pillows, adding sparkle and light throughout the room, like a dancing gypsy's skirt.

Amid the color and pattern, two key pieces of furniture in rich, dark wood ground the room. One, a traditional rosewood bureau inlaid with shimmering mother-of-pearl and adds a familial warm touch to the room, as does the other, an antique apothecary chest. Bold writing identifies the exotic herbs that used to be kept inside its drawers hundreds of years ago. Today it is transformed into an oversized jewelry box and writing desk.

FOLLOWING PAGES: Piles of pink, pattern, and texture create a bohemian escape in this bedroom. Fabrics take center stage as layers of leopard, paisley, flowers, and stripes cover almost every surface, adding both softness and intrigue.

Diversity of design continues with the white, beige, and pink area rug and multicolored lamps that dangle alluringly from within the canopy bed's cove. The bed's closable colorful curtains, as flirty and flowing as a Mathew Williamson tunic, infuse the bed with drama and embellish the room's bohemian charm.

Here, free-spirited bohemian style and a soft, romantic mystique create a timeless enclave for unwinding or planning a new escapade.

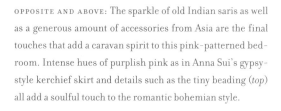

OPPOSITE AND ABOVE: The sparkle of old Indian saris as well as a generous amount of accessories from Asia are the final touches that add a caravan spirit to this pink-patterned bedroom. Intense hues of purplish pink as in Anna Sui's gypsy-style kerchief skirt and details such as the tiny beading (*top*) all add a soulful touch to the romantic bohemian style.

## |ECO ECLECTIC| natural instincts

AS YOU ENTER THIS SMALL, WOODY HOUSE, the unexpected merges elegantly with all things green, good, and glamorous in the eco and eclectic kitchen. Here, highly sustainable function meets inviting, collected design. Like a recycled pair of chunky cork wedge-heeled shoes from the seventies, this kitchen takes influences from modern and vintage while celebrating the home owner's love and respect for earth-friendly and organic materials.

Just as cutting-edge fashion designer Koi Suwannagate upgrades the concept of recycling by turning vintage cashmere into sculptural fabric embellishments, kitchen designer Karen Harautuneian does the same in this house. Her kitchen is a study in stylish sustainability, where the goal is to achieve natural balance without sacrificing comfort or taste.

eco eclectic

With eco style, reuse of raw materials is paramount. A local furniture maker used reclaimed teakwood to create Karen's countertop, fireplace, and shelves. Natural and untreated American wood used for basic construction puts an emphasis on eco responsibility with unsealed pine panels for the walls and American oak timber floors. Raw metals like bronze, brass, and stainless steel accent the room, creating a luminous glow with their natural patina. Custom linen curtains hang languorously from 1940s wood rings, brackets, and a bamboo rod.

In this space, which feels like a kitchen and family room in one, Karen could just as easily host a dinner party for a group of twenty as she could an intimate coffee with girlfriends. Thanks to a hefty, large rectangular wooden table that serves triple duty as an extra prep station, room divider, and central space in which to sit and eat, the kitchen remains open and friendly.

Walk through the exterior Dutch door and a steady stream of light and air comes with you. With windows and doors purposefully oriented to take full advantage of natural light and cool breezes, the space requires no air-conditioning. The small-footprint lifestyle of an eco home contributes to low energy use overall.

Furnishings and accessories in both the kitchen and connecting family room have shapely, curvy silhouettes that balance the straight lines in all of the wood and bring a sense of fun to the space. For example, a trio of hourglass-shaped leather and chrome chairs sit at the kitchen table, while a curvy rosewood Eames chair rests in the family area. To further tie the two spaces together, Karen reupholstered the Eames in almost-black aubergine leather that echoes the stain of the kitchen's lower cabinets. Next to the Eames, a curvaceous hula girl lamp, complete with an eco raffia grass skirt, is topped by a circular 1950s lamp shade. A shaggy Scandinavian wool rug sits at the center of the room, the result of a trade-in for two previously owned rugs. The fluffy texture adds another element of whimsy.

The entire abode follows in the footsteps of ecologically conscious designers who find gems in junk shops and crowded marketplaces and repurpose them into new designs. Karen sought out one-of-a-kind items with personality aplenty, and made them work together as only she could do.

The kitchen cabinets reference both modern simplicity and traditional clean lines, complementing the modern forms of the kitchen table

A charming collection of old still-life and farm-animal oil paintings artfully covers most of Karen's back wall of painted white planks in her kitchen-cum-living area. As well as creating the illusion of windows above her kitchen sink, the group of paintings visually connects the living room with the kitchen.

and chairs. The simple cabinets also deliver a neutral backdrop for a gallery of vintage oil paintings, many of which Karen found while shopping in Paris and London flea markets and locally, near her home.

This eco-friendly kitchen pushes the three R's—reduce, reuse, and recycle—to an elevated level of creativity and design sophistication. The room doesn't reproduce one style, but rather, in true eco and eclectic form, is a happy reflection of Karen's energetic and eco-conscious personality, always open, earthy, and bright.

Karen's woodsy kitchen stays light and open thanks to a whitewashed window seat and nook area where one can draw the ivory linen curtains and be secluded from the kitchen clatter or keep them open and be part of the action. Byblos mixes an earthy palette with a bohemian, layered spirit. Karen's judicious use of her favorite shade of pear yellow in key accessories in the kitchen and in her wardrobe reflects her sunny disposition.

## |CASUAL ROMANTIC| bouquet fresh

AT FIRST BLUSH, THE CONCEPT OF A ROMANTIC living space's working with the day-in, day-out practicality needed for a family room sounds like a pipe dream. But in this welcoming, pink-hued room, form and function live harmoniously. With a family of six running in and out—the family's junior members are all under eleven—practicality must be an integral part of the room, while prettiness remains paramount.

Three of the home owners' four children are girls, so delicate colors outnumber harsher tones in this easy yet elegant family room. Just as a pair of pink ballet shoes instantly upgrades a pair of worn jeans, the room uses tonal soft shades of pink, cream, gold, silver, and green to achieve similar results. Unusual accessories with a story to tell, in the form of old books, heirloom silver, and a collection of vases, keep things interesting and lively, and function as easy conversation pieces for visitors young and old.

casual romantic

Backing the bookshelves, the home owner has hung a delicate floral period wallpaper of rosy bouquet hues, which adds a touch of elegance, like an exotic Vivienne Tam blouse does to a basic cream suit. Framed by the white shelves, the wallpaper pattern is subtle—just enough to avoid overwhelming the space with excessive formality.

A subtle touch of silver in the wallpaper nicely ties to the home owner's mercury glass collection. Scattered throughout the room, these collectibles—vases, candlesticks, frames, and spheres—offer a shimmer from the nineteenth century.

One of the family room's focal points is on the fireplace mantel, a bright bouquet still life painted by a family friend, in a gold frame. While the oil painting has a certain formality, the casual family photographs balance it with reminders of those who live in the home. Flanking the bouquet oil painting, gold candlesticks add a touch of glamour while balancing out the mantel vignette. Furthering the gold accents is the collection of old books with gold leaf embossed on their spines, suggesting a

FOLLOWING PAGES: The subtle textures in the white wood-paneled walls, the wallpaper inside the built-in bookcases, the sisal rug over the wide-plank floors, and the linen fabrics and leather pouf keep the pastel and flowery palette of this living room interesting.

ABOVE AND OPPOSITE: Rosy embellishments used in fashion, such as Elie Saab did on his neutral petticoat-inspired dress, work just as well in home decor. Silk lavender velvet, pale pink linen, old crystal, and mercury glass all tell a quiet textural story in this pale-hued living room.

casual library-cum-salon mood, while encouraging kids to leaf through a few.

The fabrics used in this family room are soft and casual, made romantic with prints and color, especially pink. Following in the fashion footsteps of young designer Erin Fetherston, who uses a girlish sensibility in her casual frocks, the decor here layers satin, velvet, and linen in a collection of decorative pillows as well as a number of contrasting textures and garden prints.

The furniture for a family room should be synonymous with user-friendly, everyday style. Here, wrapping the armchair and a pair of love seats in soft pink and floral linen slipcovers with tiny ruffle trim is a romantic approach with a sensible twist. The slipcovers can be easily removed and laundered.

A large cream ottoman doubles as a coffee table, dressed up with a silver tray and an armful of fragrant garden flowers plopped in a pewter urn. Continuing the romantic and casual family room's floral theme, colorful jade bouquets are nestled in the built-in bookcases acting as the room's jewel.

Large French doors welcome fresh air and an even fresher concept: an open-door policy where laid-back and luxury happily coexist. Like a vintage tulle gown worn casually with gold flip-flops, it's the mix of casual and romantic that keeps this room bouquet-fresh.

## |ECLECTIC MODERN| life imitates art

WITH ITS IDIOSYNCRATIC ART JUXTAPOSED against a simple white backdrop, this dining room looks more like an art gallery than a place to eat and gather with friends. A quirky blend of original iconic art pieces and an independent spirit unites the eclectic and modern styles found in this 1950s house.

The vision of Ray, an art gallery owner, the pieces in his house are the result of his continuing love of travel, art, and craftsmanship. Traveling the world to keep his gallery well stocked with a diverse collection of exclusive and eclectic material puts him in a fortunate and fulfilling position. On the road, choosing art for both his gallery and his home is a fluid experience as collectibles move seamlessly from the gallery space to Ray's house. Most important, there isn't one style that dominates his home. He chooses what he likes and lives with it.

Just like the fashion-forward designers Ray frequently wears—Yohji Yamamoto, Comme des Garçons, Martin Margiela—when it comes to his home, he gravitates toward the innovative. If the

eclectic modern

design elements of the home decor are clean and distinctive, they're apt to be incorporated into his living space.

His minimalist dining room, located at the center of the house, is flooded with light. In order to accommodate family and friends, a large round table is an absolute necessity, providing an atmosphere where no one feels left out. Here, that communal sensibility is care of a clean white Eero Saarinen table, a streamlined classic tulip-shaped model popularized in 1956. Around the pristine white table sit six bentwood Arne Jacobsen Series 7 chairs, one of the most copied chairs of the modern era. The chairs' warm wood shades complement the shiny white table while offering iconic design and comfort.

The room's conversation piece is the oversized anatomical model of a bee. In hand-painted plaster on its original stand, it was once gazed upon by curious science students in Belgium in the very early twentieth century. Not to be taken seriously, it adds whimsy and wonder to the room, just as a pair of avant-garde futuristic sneakers takes the seriousness out of a man's suit.

This work table, dining table, and conversation area display home owner Ray's curatorial talents of art collecting as each piece—the bee sculpture, wooden model, oil painting, and giant tree photograph—relates to the others in color, composition, and wit.

ABOVE AND OPPOSITE: Ray's preference for soft, warm, and patinaed textures is shown in his velvet coats, worn suede boots, an old oil painting, and wooden figure—all showing a certain softness or passage of time.

A tiny artist's model sits on the ledge above a traditional painting of a woman looking toward the verdant large canvas on the opposite wall. Understated in size and construction, it is handmade from wood, except for one bronze forearm. The juxtaposition of the diminutive wooden model and the larger traditional oil portrait facing a still larger giant-sized photo-landscape illustrates just how witty Ray's curatorial talents, even for his home, can be.

In addition to providing artistic contrast to the other well-chosen pieces, the statement-making "Tree Dwellers," by Anthony Goicolea, acts as an outdoor view against a solid wall. This broad window-sized photograph brings the outside in and gives the illusion that we're looking at a giant verdant tree hiding an unusual suburban house and figures of people. The massive photograph is both beautiful and edgy, while also relating to the room.

Underfoot, a low-maintenance polished cement floor is practical and smart, while continuing Ray's industrial-strength artistic attitude. Just like a pair of shoes by iconic eclectic-modernist fashion designer Dries Van Noten, the calm gray floors are built to last.

Here in Ray's room for dining, working, and contemplating the art that surrounds, he shows us that eclecticism does not have to be cluttered. In fact, this room beautifully shows how a razor-sharp mind can curate a relaxing, eclectic, and modern living space.

# |RETRO RESORT| summer camp

MIX A PALE MAI TAI PINK WITH 1950S POLY-nesian charm, add a dash of kitsch, and you've got the recipe for interior designer Jill Hall's retro-resort-styled kitchen and dining area.

As you transition from the Hall family's cool modern living room into the effervescence that is the kitchen, it's clear that color is king. A custom mix of shell-pink paint, a shade that could easily be named "carefree conch," gives the walls and original cabinets a glow. The green, yellow, and aqua accents are the familiar yet welcoming colors of resort-style living.

Like Lilly Pulitzer's favorite color palette, opening one of the original pink cabinet doors is an entrée into a world of summers from a bygone era. Brown coconut-shaped cups for a poolside cocktail share space with petite pink glasses for a swig of fresh OJ and hula girl glasses that make simple sips of water all the more fun. Like accessorizing a dress with an original seventies Bakelite bracelet found at a flea market, collecting drinking glasses is a nice way to accessorize your kitchen with good old-fashioned icons.

retro resort

Hall brings the spontaneity and fun of a last-minute picnic to her family's dining area with her choice of dining table: a sassy green picnic bench set with chic, no-nonsense galvanized aluminum wrapping the top. Not only does it add a vacation style to her space, it serves as an industrial-strength and flexible family dining table. Backyard barbecues can happen at a moment's notice with a couple of helping hands to move the set outside. Much like a crisp white linen shirt, the picnic table can transform in a flash to serve a multitude of functions. This table is an artist's "studio" for the kids to spread out on, a games table for the family, a late-night "office" for Mom's laptop, or, of course, an early-morning coffee spot. All the ways the family enjoys the newly appointed picnic bench make this corner of the house one of the most vibrant and useful.

Other useful accoutrements of this retro-tropical kitchen are the high-quality reproduction appliances, which do their job of both functioning beautifully for today and keeping their down-home charm of yesteryear. Here, the 1950s-inspired refrigerator and toaster fit right into the retro mix.

A well-edited collection of a bold, Gauguin- or Matisse-inspired kids' paintings for the fridge, a large-scaled sunny yellow lemonade jar, and a cookie jar are the three key accessories for this pale pink and white kitchen, lending it tropical color, scale, and a youthful kick.

OPPOSITE AND ABOVE: The orange and white Creamsicle light fixture above the family picnic bench along with the giant retro tiki hut poster give the eating area bold graphic appeal, just as the row of silhouetted parrot plates ties in the bright pastel palette. A picnic-ready Pucci blouse offers plenty of pink, pattern, and freedom of movement, just as Jill Hall's kitchen does.

Accessories such as cheerful melamine dishes have come back into vogue with full force, thanks to the hip and bright color choices available on the market. From local Chinatown shops to more mainstream and upscale retailers, melamine plates have come out of the picnic basket and onto this busy family's kitchen shelves. A little tiki goes a long way for accessorizing: bamboo-handled silverware is both resort-style and an ecological solution. The freshly cut torch ginger in a clear glass pitcher for the table centerpiece is another easy way to add color. A potted palm offers contrast and graphic zip to the billowing white curtains in the room's breezy corner, lending a lasting note of tropical tranquillity and fun, which is the essence of a retro-resort life.

ER HEAD AND DREAMED OF ALL THE
W WHY ARE YOU SO FAR AWAY SHE SAID
OVE WITH YOU THAT IM IN LOVE WITH
LONELY YOU STRANGE AS ANGELS
TING IN THE WATER YOURE JUST LIKE
LIGHT LICKED ME INTO SHAPE I MUST
G LIPS TO BREATHE HER NAME I OPENE
E ALONE ALONE ABOVE A RAGING SEA
DROWNED HER DEEP INSIDE OF ME YOU
YOU JUST LIKE HEAVEN

## |BOHEMIAN MODERN| the artist's way

WITH ITS STARK WHITE BACKDROP AND A wide range of art and ethnic influences, this light-filled living space blends the best of everything bohemian and modern designs have to offer—and in a big, big way.

An art dealer, the owner likes to describe her home as "Schindler House meets the ranch." The room aptly mimics a famous Schindler original, in both its large live/work-style space and its minimalist fireplace. Ranch-style details include the tongue-and-groove wood-beamed ceiling, which the home owner modernized with a coat of gallery-white paint, and a nice row of clean glass doors, which lead out to the back garden. This artful pairing of contemporary and tribal creates a warm and spacious environment for a family with two young sons, six dogs, three birds, and a cat.

Walking into this contemporary house is akin to walking into the Guggenheim-inspired white flagship Prada store in New York, or the minimalist-yet-monolithic white Hempel Hotel in London. Voluminous white space with

bohemian modern

polished concrete floors offers a gallery-like canvas on which to display gigantic-scaled bohemian pieces and statement-making art and accessories.

The biggest statement is the huge, living-room-filling suzani-covered square ottoman, which serves as a bohemian stand-in for all traditional and perhaps more fussy furnishings. This living room's biggest message is what it has not—no sofa, no coffee table, no side tables—no kidding! The soulful and tribal red and brown pattern on the giant suzani beckons you to come, lie down, and stay awhile, just as a giant primitive pattern found on a Jean Paul Gaultier or Kenzo piece invites the wearer to have a little fun. Perhaps it's because the large ottoman is positioned next to a warm and welcoming fireplace that looks as though it is used every night. It could be because of the primitive brown cushions on the concrete built-in benches right next to the fireplace that also serve as firewood storage. Either way, the primitive touches seem to hit all who enter at a gut level, just as good art can capture an appreciative eye, and they keep the family in the living space for hours on end.

As bold and brave as its modern and boho underpinnings are, the space also makes room for practicality. Family and pets can move easily between indoors and outdoors with wide-swinging doors on either side of the room, which encourage an effortless, communal flow. The dining area, which offers a continuous interplay of old and new, is a spacious gathering place for family and friends. An antique barn table imported from a farm in Ireland feels as comfy as a warm cashmere sweater. On one side of the table, seating is no-fuss in the form of a simple Cubist bench. On the table's other side is a quartet of fluid Panton chairs. Crafted from one piece of plastic, they are as stylized as an eye-catching bag by modern fashion icon Custo Barcelona. An abstract still life anchors the dining room, and overhead hanging glass globe pendants—reproductions inspired by Eichler's midcentury modern original—add a glowing string of light.

Like a well-traveled gypsy and a well-healed doyenne who've become fast friends, the room combines playfulness and formality, old and new. A character-rich urn found at a flea market sits below a piece of bold modern art, recalling the perfect blend of a Tocca sari dress with a brand-new patent pump. An Indonesian drum provides an exclamation point beneath the large, lyrical dream canvas. Vaulted barn ceilings and French doors provide endless air and light, and

A broad poetic canvas of graphic type sits above the fireplace, inviting the viewer to read and reread the dreamy words; while a monolithic suzani ottoman beckons you to lounge and contemplate in the gallery-like living area.

Inside the artwork on the wall, the text reads:

SHOW ME SHOW ME SHOW ME HOW YOU DO THAT TRICK THE ONE
ME SCREAM SHE SAID THE ONE THAT MAKES ME LAUGH SHE SAID
R ARMS AROUND MY NECK SHOW ME HOW YOU DO IT AND I PROMISE
E THAT ILL RUN AWAY WITH YOU ILL RUN AWAY WITH YOU SPINNING
Y EDGE I KISSED HER FACE AND KISSED HER HEAD AND DREAMED
DIFFERENT WAYS I HAD TO MAKE HER GLOW WHY ARE YOU SO FAR
WHY WONT YOU EVER KNOW THAT IM IN LOVE WITH YOU THAT IM I
YOU YOU SOFT AND ONLY YOU LOST AND LONELY YOU STRANGE A
DANCING IN THE DEEPEST OCEANS TWISTING IN THE WATER YOU
A DREAM YOURE JUST LIKE A DREAM DAYLIGHT LICKED ME INTO
HAVE BEEN ASLEEP FOR DAYS AND MOVING LIPS TO BREATHE HER
ED UP MY EYES AND FOUND MYSELF ALONE ALONE ALONE ABOVE
THAT STOLE THE ONLY GIRL I LOVED AND DROWNED HER DEEP INS
J SOFT AND ONLY YOU LOST AND LONELY YOU JUST LIKE HEAVEN

"The dining area, which offers a continuous interplay of old and new, is a spacious gathering place for family and friends."

like a flexible, go-with-everything pair of boots, the polished concrete floor delivers pragmatism and understated style.

Ready for any event, from an impromptu art show to a down-home family meal, this bohemian yet modern room takes on the energy of both the old and the new and blends it as only an artist can do, with big, bold brushstrokes for high impact and personal style.

OPPOSITE AND ABOVE: Large scale, simple forms, and tribal touches are what unite this dining area of naïf artwork and suzani textiles; the influences can be found in the fashions of Christian Lacroix and Diane von Furstenberg.

## |RESORT CASUAL| safe harbor

FOR THE OWNERS OF THIS MARIN COUNTY home, escape comes in the form of their very own Martha's Vineyard–inspired cabana. After battling the San Francisco workweek, once back home, they have this casual-resort-style retreat in the heart of Tiburon to escape to. This family enjoys a no-plan-necessary backyard getaway 365 days a year. And they do it in classic marina style.

A nautical theme gives the room all the appeal of carefree summer days aboard a clean-as-a-whistle ship. Drenched in all-American red, white, and blue, the design may be as traditional as a pair of original Sperry Top-Sider boat shoes, but the innovative floor plan is quintessential northern California. Here, there is no separation between indoors and outdoors. Only floor-to-ceiling accordion doors separate an oversized great room overlooking the bay from the pool. The result is a polished style and casual sophistication, with all the accoutrements of a five-star resort.

Tank, Moschino, $215, at Bergdorf Goodman, NYC

Linen shor... at MaxMa...

Canvas wedge, Christian Louboutin, $310,

Sunglass... D&G, $... at D&G napharma...

Dsquared

resort casual

Gray shingles are in the style of a classic Cape Cod, a type of colonial home typically covered in hand-split wood shingles left unpainted to weather naturally. The ocean theme is carried indoors with a celebration of coastal maritime life. Nautical accents like hurricane lamps, navy and white life preservers, sailboat models, and ship windows on the changing-room doors leave little room for interpretation. This is a place where the love of the sea is apparent.

The floor is covered with sisal, which is perfect for high-traffic entertaining and slippery wet feet. Two oversized chairs dressed in traditional seashell-printed slips flank the crisp white sofa adorned with navy-and-white-striped accent cushions. A wet bar waits for the crew to arrive and a kitchenette is all that is needed to create a light dinner or party fare. A wide wooden ladder leads to the upstairs loft, which is a perfect hideaway and a relaxing spot in which to read or nap.

Punctuating the exterior of the great room are traditional white columns atop stone bases. Just steps beyond these columns outside is another opportunity to relax, on a set of outdoor lounge chairs covered in bright red Sunbrella, a rich, high-performance fabric that resists fading and repels water. Their generous scale encourages poolside visitors to kick off their shoes and relax. An upscale four-course dinner

would work just as well on the boxy, well-placed picnic table as would hamburgers and hot dogs.

With its celebration of fresh, salty air, it comes as no surprise that this very grown-up cabana blends the first-cabin polish details of resort living with the casual attitude of the home owners and their choice of easy-care slips and fabrics. This is carried over in the outdoor shower as well. All shades of sea and sky blues are reflected in the tiny mosaic shower tiles, while a whitewashed shingle door continues the seaside serendipity.

ABOVE AND RIGHT: Kenzo makes the most of the nautical trio of red, white, and cream by adding the charm of ropey mac-ramé in his resort collection, much like this interior uses sisal grass-cloth as a barefoot-friendly flooring as well as the same universally appealing flag palette.

Reminiscent of a classic seaside home on the rocky bluffs of New England, this charming combo of cabana and great room mixes a come-as-you-are style with classic sensibilities. There's no need to travel far when the resort is waiting for you right in your own backyard.

Classic East Coast cabana style makes this house feel like the home owners are living in a year-round resort with graphic nautical touches, such as the navy-and-white-striped accessories, old ships, and buoys to keep one's eye afloat. Lacoste, a perennial classic sport brand, offers the same breezy white-on-white easy elegance made popular in the 1920s.

# | CLASSIC COUTURE | a formal affair

A MÉLANGE OF CLASSIC AND COUTURE STYLES, this dining room could just as easily be located in a French château as in a pied-à-terre on Park Avenue. The room is like the perfect little black dress, beautifully cut and the very essence of elegance.

The world of couture fashion demands an artisanal approach to superlative handcraftsmanship and an expert finessing of fabric and trim. Classic designs withstand the test of time. With this dining room, interior designer Elizabeth Dinkel accomplishes a celebration of both styles. It's a place where Christian Lacroix and Ralph Lauren could have a seat at the table. In this custom-designed dining room, opulence pairs with understatement in a perfect assembly of pedigreed antiques with handmade details.

No detail goes unattended in this dining room, starting with the stunning custom-colored de Gournay wallpaper on Indian tea paper. Just as handmade signifies couture, this hand-painted paper adds a magical garden of dazzling detail and fanciful imagery of an

"Everybody thinks white's

"Choose a color for the

BENJAMIN MOORE
HORIZON OC-53

cktail ring

classic couture

OPPOSITE AND ABOVE: Classicism and formality rule in this classic couture dining room; one enters through an elevated arch and approaches a Chippendale mahogany table flanked by a pair of floor-to-ceiling windows, which invite the diners gaze to the garden beyond. Jade-green garden-inspired wallpaper further invites guests to imagine their meals taken under the stars.

imagined China popular with European monarchs like Louis XV. Originally designed to imitate Chinese porcelain, here the birds, leaves, and branches set against leafy green simply serve as a calming backdrop for a night of fine dining. Like the gold accent on a Dior dress, a classic Regency-style mirror, circa 1815, hung over the fireplace accents the wallpaper's gold touch. Ornamented with a carved eagle topper, this style of convex mirror, popular in the late eighteenth century, represents classic British style. A glass Louis IV Bagues sconce rests on either side, also playing up the wallpaper's delicate spring tones. The classically detailed curtains, featuring a creamy, classic Greek key design against an ivory blend of wool and silk, frame the oversized French doors that lead to the outdoor patio.

European craftsmanship welcomes visitors on the entry floor in the form of custom-cut black and white Belgian stone. The classic harlequin pattern of the floor leading into the dining room adds dignity and contrast, like a handsome host in a classic tuxedo. The old Parisian marble of the fireplace, an antique French crystal chandelier, and an heirloom pair of sterling candlesticks poised tall on the dining room table all add ageless appeal. With its gilt and sparkling droplets of crystal, the chandelier, like a classic piece of Van Cleef & Arpels

CLOCKWISE FROM ABOVE LEFT: Couture and classic details in this dining room include hand-embroidered drapes in a classic oversize key pattern done in tone-on-tone cream satin, while the sparkle of the sconces above the fireplace recall the couture one-of-a-kind detailing found in Oscar de la Renta's more sedate green and black collection and in vintage jewels.

jewelry, is a particularly striking centerpiece for the room.

Exquisitely carved Chippendale chairs, a style that dominated American furniture in the eighteenth century and endures today, complement the matching Chippendale table. The rich mahogany, considered by Thomas Chippendale to be the easiest to carve, and the only wood he used, offers a deep contrast to the rest of the room's light tones, and is as sumptuous as a soft leather coat.

A sand-toned area rug of sisal, known for its durability, is the only sign of everyday pragmatism in a room otherwise designed for special occasions. Custom-made for the room, however, even the rug has its own upgrade: it features a custom-colored linen binding in true couture style. The sisal's natural texture keeps the rest of the room from feeling too stuffy.

The key to unlocking couture-classic style in this home comes to sparkling life in the painstaking details offered in its choice antiques, and in its application of archetypal design principles of scale, proportion, and balance. Because of its impeccable craftsmanship and serene homage to nature, this dining room manages to look effortless, in spite of the tremendous detail that went into creating it. It's an unforced and timeless style that requires a studied discipline of design to achieve its fabulously unstudied look.

# |ECLECTIC BOHEMIAN| rhythm and blues

HE'S ORIGINALLY FROM NEW YORK, SHE FROM Oklahoma, and together they've laid down some deep roots in an old Craftsman bungalow out West. With piles of eclectic home decor fueled by their shared bohemian spirit and love of music, they've filled an intimate eight hundred square feet of space with a montage of eclectic cool. Think of mixing a denim prairie skirt with a pair of beat-up cowboy boots and a vintage rocker T, and you'll understand the inspiration behind this room's decor.

A deep shade of peacock-blue paint envelops the room, and was inspired by a sculpture of a colorful bird found at a flea market. Tamed with ochre, brown, white, and woods, this typical West Coast bungalow looks well lived in. Whether the scene of an afternoon snooze, a jam session with friends, or a "tour" of the musical memorabilia for late-night listeners, the room oozes with rhythm-and-blues cool. Janis Joplin, dressed rocker-style in corduroy hip huggers and a pin-tucked white blouse, would fit in just fine here.

eclectic bohemian

When decorating with opposites, anything goes. Hand-me-down leather cowboy boots, a midnight-black Moroccan pouf, and heaps of music books and vinyl records all scattered around the honey-hued wood floor work well to bring the couple's shared love of collecting and music together in soulful harmony. Boundless in its energy, the room includes reverberating pattern play from the giant ochre-and-golden-hued paisley curtains to the vintage graphic old Western blanket on the Danish modern sofa. A few cowhide patterns, one on the floor found on eBay and another on a chair, continue the pattern play with an emphasis on the rocker-meets-cowgirl spirit. Another pattern, found in the orange paisley scarf, drapes from a microphone used for impromptu recording sessions, Steven Tyler–style. Many more scarves and patterns are available in the home owner's closet, depending on how she'd like to accent that corner of the room, or what mood the vocalist is in. Living room, closet, recording studio—like a gypsy wagon, everything here works together and is an evolving collage.

Amid the ever-rotating cast of characters in decor or visitors, a crisp white wall of typical

Music takes center stage in this young couple's Craftsman bungalow as instruments and musical paraphernalia serve as both entertainment and decor.

Craftsman built-ins provides contrast and order to the freewheeling room. Books fill the attractive prairie-styled glass cabinets that flank a generous number of drawers, keeping the collectors in check on what they choose to display and what they choose to stow away. Resting atop the cabinets are large-scale posters and photographs of music and fashion icons such as Bob Dylan, Jimi Hendrix, and The Beatles. In addition to giving the room yet another layer of personality, it's the large scale and proportion of the accessories along the main storage wall that make the room work.

The final touches are the accessories— peacock feathers, old brass candlesticks, and musical instruments picked up over the years— that serve double duty as entertainment as well as decor.

From the rich blue, brown, and gold color scheme to the mix of pattern and piles of collections, this combination of eclectic and bohemian styles provides this young couple a creative and spirited canvas on which to build.

## |RETRO CASUAL| cooking with color

THERE'S NO DOUBT ABOUT IT. THE KITCHEN is the hardest-working room in the house. But there's no need to put aside fun while preparing a meal, loading the dishwasher, or going over the day's game plan with the kids. Fun is the norm in this casual-and-retro-styled kitchen for a family of six. Its simple Shaker-style cabinetry and wide wood-plank floors offer a great backdrop for a little over-the-top retro accessorizing to get the place hopping.

Cherry red, bubble-gum pink, and vibrant turquoise coat almost every accessory in this pristine white kitchen, giving it an energetic retro style reminiscent of the 1950s. The most energy emanates from a swingin' set of lipstick-red plastic stools resembling three shiny patent-leather heels. The stools keep counter guests swirling, and can be cleaned with the swipe of a sponge. Their shiny round chrome bases offer sturdy support for little ones, while at the same time recalling the chrome hubcap of

retro casual

a classic fifties race car. On the large white-paneled Sub-Zero fridge, two huge old metal ice cream store signs perk up the entire space. In true pop-art form, an oversized strawberry ice cream cone sits next to another equally huge strawberry ice cream sundae, adding color and wit from a bygone era. Magnet-mounting these collectible signs onto the refrigerator's wood-paneled doors allow something old and charming to be used in a creative way, furthering the kitchen's retro and casual appeal.

The six-foot island in the middle of the room is the heart of the kitchen. Kids can color, Mom can bake, and Dad can work on fixing his latest gadget, with room to spare, on an easy-to-clean Carrera marble countertop. The gray-veined marble is also reminiscent of an old soda-fountain counter, inspiring the family's own impromptu ice cream parties. Wide drawer storage and deep counter space make at-your-fingertips storage easy. Brightening up the island's center is a ballerina-pink and brown polka-dot table runner, while a schoolhouse-style Pullman lamps glow above it like a dangling pendant.

Although the bright and punchy accessories

FOLLOWING PAGES: The clean, white Shaker-style kitchen with warm wood floors and Carrera marble countertops is the perfect casual background for retro reds, aquas, and pinks sprinkled into all of its accessories.

OPPOSITE AND ABOVE: It's the colorful and quirky touches, such as a beautiful old O'Keefe and Merritt range from the 1940s, a polka-dotted apron, and hand-labeled jars of gumballs and taffy, that liven up this all-white kitchen, just as old colorful buttons and wild tartan brights from Missoni keep one's wardrobe lively.

in this open and casual kitchen give off a not-so-serious air, when it comes to actual cooking, the chef is in luck thanks to its dreamy old range oven, pristinely restored. The 1940s O'Keefe and Merritt oven is both a major collectible and a highlight of the room, with four ovens and six burners—on which even the most jaded of chefs would love to work.

Just as bright patent shoes and accessories can enliven a closet full of neutrals, candy-colored dishes punch up this whipped-cream-white kitchen. More colorful details, including a pink blender, a bright-red food scale, and green-striped blinds, add an optimistic energy to this kitchen, proving that having a retro-styled kitchen is only a few bright accessories away.

# |MODERN CLASSIC| compact chic

THE BRILLIANT JUXTAPOSITION OF MODERN and classic design styles vibrates through this chic and compact studio apartment. Designed for a young woman with joie-de-vivre sensibilities, the studio is at once provocative and comfortable.

As a fashion stylist, Hannah has many diverging influences. Part classic and part modern, Hannah's personal style is evident throughout this well-mannered living space. Distinctive contemporary design aesthetics are softened with traditional elements that suggest Hollywood Regency glamour with the wit of a David Hicks apartment.

The design challenge faced by interior designer Mark Cole was to transform a twenty-by-forty-foot studio into a place to live, eat, sleep, and entertain. He elegantly resolved the problem through the use of design-savvy compartmentalization. Each area is clearly defined by bold strokes of color. A black area rug outlines the dining area, while a contrasting white area rug represents the borders for the lounge. The yellow bench at the foot of the bed adds a

modern classic

feminine touch with its curling legs, and clearly delineates the end of one space and the start of the next.

The high-contrast tricolor palette of canary yellow, white, and black creates an energetic ambience. The broad presence of white makes the accents pop brilliantly yet is shrewdly balanced by the natural shade of the woven sisal and the pale gray of the wall behind the bed. This room is like a pret-a-porter Paris runway show, classically tailored, but done in attention-grabbing motifs, color, and texture. Because the use of color is tamed with grounding elements, the room manages to coexist as both a living space and a design statement.

Contrast is at the heart of the design, and outlines and piping form another of the room's consistent design motifs. The brilliant white pillows of the couch are squared off in a thick black stroke while the throw pillows are of a hatched yellow bamboo pattern. Shiny outlines continue into the dining area, where a slick black finish on the chairs frames white vinyl upholstery.

Dramatic hand-screened black and white wallpaper, beautifully featured on an accent wall, brings a graphic and natural element to the space. In this treatment, a traditional Audubon motif is reinterpreted in striking silhouette. The studio feels open and airy thanks to the wallpaper's design, which evokes space and nature. The large mirror in the dining area is another way to make a confined space feel bigger—it reflects the accent wall, so the room seems to go on and on.

From contemporary nightstands in high gloss, with their matching yellow and black lamps, to the careful stacks of lacquer boxes, the room is precisely balanced, infusing the classical dictum of order and stability like a pair of classic quilted Chanel ballet flats. This equilibrium helps to provide steadiness to what could otherwise be an overwhelmingly vibrant design. Looking more closely across the room, other evidence of classicism soon appears—the Greek key motif on the side table is echoed in the fabric of the black throw pillows on the bed; while a pair of dangling birdcages nod to the formal architecture of Eastern pagodas.

The elegant union of modern and classic styles continues in several well-chosen pieces rich in contrast: a tabletop Italian Grand Stallion statue in deeply glazed ceramic; classic Louis XVI dining chairs, usually in gold leaf, fashioned with glossy black paint; a white circular dining table, with its traditional pedestal base; and regal lamps topped with tailored black

A long, oval mirror-topped cocktail table serves as the perfect place to showcase Hannah's collections or prop her feet, and it reflects the vibrant color palette of the room.

silk shades next to a table with a coat of yellow paint over a classic urn base.

Equal parts entertainment, comfort, and elegance, this studio is reminiscent of one of fashion's icons, Audrey Hepburn, exuding her happy-go-lucky, Holly Golightly charm. A completely new spin on the average one-room studio, this sunny design combines modernity with classic foundations. The outcome is fun, fresh, and fabulous.

OPPOSITE AND ABOVE: The black-and-white tree-lined wallpaper serves as a mood-enhancing pop-art meadow for both Hannah and her visitors. The vertical lines also help to uplift and enlarge the diminutive studio apartment. Coco Chanel and Badgley Mischka are two ready-to-wear designers who happily employ black and white in new ways, season after season, just as this apartment's crisp palette will look fresh for years to come.

# |VINTAGE ROMANTIC| secondhand rose

ROMANCE, BOTH OLD AND NEW, INFUSES THE living room in Michelle's petite yet style-packed home. In this multifunctional space in a house where space is at a premium, everything is repurposed and reimagined with a sweet vintage and romantic style. An office, dining room, and cozy family room are all wrapped up in a mix-and-match whirl of beauty and history.

As a prop stylist, Michelle is intimately familiar with antiques and the place they can hold in our hearts. In fact, her own home acts as a key prop room, one she often raids to decorate interiors or sets for various photo or film shoots. The room's white paint allows for easy transitions as Michelle searches for replacements and switches the furniture and accessories around, just as a plain white linen dress can offer a nice background for an ever-changing collection of old jewels and accessories.

The thrill of the hunt in Michelle's job keeps
this home always in a state of cheery flux. A trip
to an old Iowa barn that is now an antique store
yielded a nice prize: a pair of brass cameo curtain
tiebacks that now keep Michelle's white linen
curtains in order. French beaded crystal chandeliers dangle from her ceilings like a favorite
pair of timeworn crystal and pearl earrings.
Servingware became wall art as Michelle artfully
hung large creamy-white and off-white old serving platters above the whitewashed dining buffet,
using a pitcher of old silverware and sterling
silver pieces on the buffet to complete the
camera-ready vignette. The patterns don't
match—a vintage aesthetic—but the oval shapes,
plates, trays, and even a bust are monochromatic
in white, off-white, and silver. The palette and
texture of Michelle's romantic vision of vintage
are much like her collection of all-white crochet
and linen heirloom dresses, light on the color but
heavy on the history and details.

Divided from the dining area by a white-
slipped sofa, the family room is centered with
an oversized rattan basket that also serves as a
coffee table. Just as an old basket served as
British style icon Jane Birkin's purse much of
the time while she shopped the streets of Paris,
this functional rattan piece in Michelle's living

vintage romantic

room does double duty as both a storage spot for her family's stuff and as a canvas for any number of accessories according to the day's needs. A generously sized serving tray on top keeps a clean and steady surface for a vase full of garden roses, or a few glasses of iced tea.

Covering the large-scale sofa is a quilted white matelassé slipcover, which can be easily thrown into the wash, and even bleached, if necessary. It also helps to enlarge the feeling of the small room and make the division between the dining room and office area pronounced. Just as a pair of tried-and-true white jeans acts as an easy and clean base to feature an ever-rotating collection of frilly floral tops and cool vintage accessories, Michelle's white sofa serves as a platform for her rotating pillow collection, which changes according to her mood. For now, a pair of humble flaxen linen pillows sits in front of a pair of nice toile pillows, with a velvet and rosy cushion plopped happily in the middle. The mix of patterns and textures keeps the space from feeling too precious.

On the windows, soft light filters through the simple white linen curtains, reminiscent of a

Unapologetically feminine details, an old crystal chandelier, a curvy white armoire, and armfuls of garden flowers all work together to add romance to Michelle's collection-filled family cottage.

flowing Grecian Madeleine Vionnet dress, which imbue the room with a romantic air. Opposite the large windows and floor-to-ceiling white curtains sits a refurbished armoire that holds the entire contents of Michelle's office. Her shingle is turned to CLOSED when the doors are shut, and the beat-up aqua paint lends a relaxing hue to the white color palette.

Finding perfect pieces and pulling them all together cohesively, Michelle continues to create a lived-in environment infused with nostalgic sparkle. It's the balance of daydreamy romanticism with real-life imperfection that makes this room so liveable and lovable.

OPPOSITE AND ABOVE: Spontaneous yet time-worn touches are what make Michelle's small cottage sing, such as the way she casually crowns this bust with found old sparkly tiaras, as if tossed on while walking by, or the way she pairs a leopard print with an old caned side chair to add some humor. Pearly earrings, looking as if they were picked up from the five-and-dime, and a petticoat dress by Blumarine recall the romantic and carefree charm of the past.

## |ECO BOHEMIAN| nomadic spirit

UPLIFTING STROKES, BOTH BROAD AND small, is the style message Paulette Cole likes to convey in her light-filled Manhattan loftlike space. Adorning our nests, and ourselves, is as primal as eating food, but according to Paulette, CEO and creative director of ABC Carpet & Home, it doesn't have to be done in a toxic way. Here, she illustrates how she walks her eco talk in the ecologically minded and bohemian-styled living space that she shares with her daughter in New York's Flatiron District.

In Paulette's space, bohemian is spelled with a capital *B*, as to her, the very essence of bohemian is not only embracing indigenous cultures and keeping alive their craftsmanship, it's also being antilabel and antistatus. The richly hued caravan-like apartment with spiritual references aplenty exudes such a self-assured spirituality, that name-dropping here would feel as bad as littering. So in her apartment, you won't find the logo or status symbols

eco bohemian

sometimes sought out by social climbers; you'll find a love of humanity, nature, and old things from someone who has already arrived and is working now to make a change in the way we decorate.

Case in point: the shell of her apartment and a few key "background" pieces, such as her undyed Sustainable Furnishings Council organic linen sofas, a tall and elegant wood sculpture behind her desk, and plain salvaged steel book/display cases are all as simple as an unadorned Dosa mandarin top, while also managing to be as nontoxic to the space and the planet as possible. With its wood floors, naturally glazed plaster walls, and diaphanous white gauzy curtains letting in the maximum amount of natural light and fresh air through four sky-filled windows, the clean and eco-conscious backdrop of the room sets the stage for the more colorful bohemian action that fills it.

Against the spare backdrop is a bohemian explosion of primitive and graphic colors taken from indigenous cultures around the world. Like armfuls of colorful shimmering bangles used to dress up an outfit, heaps of colorful furnishings, each with a story to tell, fill Paulette's natural loft space. Believing that the world of retail is becoming too homogenized, Paulette is passionate about using intensely colored and naturally dyed textiles, furnishings, and accessories to enrich our spaces. Rich reds in the form of a large primitive rug underneath her living area mix with modern scarlet in a recycled plastic modern desk chair, while a kaleidoscope of color is found in religious objects intentionally placed around the room. For example, above the eco and neutral sofa, an extra large Nepalese Buddhist Mandala Romeo textile shimmers with uplifting detail and craftsmanship while holding a place of importance as the focal point of the room. Just as Donna Karan uses spiritual and tribal symbols in decorative and message-sending ways for her Urban Zen collection, so does Paulette, with her Indian Ganesha mini shrine on her recycled modern steel bookcase illuminated by old amber votives.

The open space around the dining room table is a clear bohemian bow to the world traveler. With access to the world, it's hard to pick just one style, so she instead joyfully parades four disparate chairs of different cultures, styles, and eras around a simple wood and stone octagonal table. Buying old pieces, to

To support her environmental mission, Paulette Cole of ABC Carpet & Home chooses to leave well enough alone in her low-impact loft, illustrated by the exposed plumbing and pipes throughout and the untreated plaster walls and wood floors.

Paulette, is the ultimate form of recycling, as she believes antiques serve as our archives of design.

This pure and lively multifunctioning space reflects all the disparate roles that the modern lady of the house plays—archivist, activist, spiritualist, and mother—with its eco-neutral background and joie-de-vivre bohemian spirit.

OPPOSITE AND ABOVE: The diaphanous gauzy curtains casually hung on raw-looking metal rods mirror the flowing gauzy ensemble of Donna Karan's runway look. Cole feathers her nest with shiny homage to cultures around the world, much like J. Lancetti adorns her natural collection with chunky jewels of color.

# design resources

ERCOLE HOME
Phone: 718-797-4270
www.ercolehome.com

F | F & S FABRICS
10629 West Pico Boulevard
Los Angeles, CA 90064
Phone: 310-475-1637
www.fandsfabrics.com

F & S FABRICS FOR THE
HOME
10654 West Pico Boulevard
Los Angeles, CA 90064
Phone: 310-441-2477
www.fandsfabrics.com

FABRICS AND PAPERS
Phone: 44-0-1403-713028
www.fabricsandpapers.com

FABRICUT, RITZ PARIS
COLLECTION
Phone: 800-999-8200
www.fabricut.com

FADED FINES ANTIQUES
2055 S. Barrington, Suite B
Los Angeles, CA 90025
Phone: 310-966-9191

FASHION THERAPY
2305 Wilshire Boulevard
Santa Monica, CA 90407
Phone: 310-264-2577

FIBREWORKS
Phone: 502-499-9944
www.fibreworks.com

G | THE G HOTEL
Phone: 353-0-91-865200
www.theghotel.ie

H | HANNAH'S TREASURES
VINTAGE WALLPAPER
COLLECTION
Phone: 866-755-3173
www.hannahstreasures.com

HILLARY CRAMER
Phone: 310-754-5090

HOUSE INC.
Phone: 310-449-1918
www.houseinc.com

HOUSE INC. BOUTIQUE
1607 Montana Avenue
Santa Monica, CA 90403
Phone: 310-451-2597
Fax: 310-451-2598
www.houseincboutique.com

HUB OF THE HOUSE
KITCHENS & INTERIORS
Karen Harautuneian
420 North Robertson
    Boulevard
Los Angeles, CA 90048
Phone: 310-652-2332
Fax: 310-652-7666

I | IL PRIMO PASSO
1624 Montana Avenue
Santa Monica, CA 90403
Phone: 310-828-4149
www.ilprimopasso.com

J | JENNIFER HOGABOAM,
STYLIST AND DESIGNER
Phone: 310-806-3958
E-mail: jhogaboam@aol.com

K | KRAVET
Phone: 800-645-9068
www.kravet.com

L | LAURA BURKHALTER
DESIGN STUDIO
6404 Hollywood Boulevard,
    Suite 328
Hollywood, CA 90028
Phone: 323-469-2021 or
    323-404-4841
Fax: 323-375-0469
E-mail: info@lb-dc.com
www.lauraburkhalter.com

LISA STRONG
Phone: 310-652-2000
www.studiocollaborative.com

LITTLE HOUSE
BOUTIQUE
1603 Montana Avenue
Santa Monica, CA 90403
Phone: 310-451-1321
Fax: 310-451-1323
www.littlehouse
    boutique.com

M | MARY HUNTSMAN ART
Phone: 310-472-4153
E-mail: maryhuntsman@
    earthlink.net
www.maryhuntsman.com

MAURA DANIEL,
LIGHTING COUTURE
Phone: 310-838-8844
Fax: 310-838-4786
E-mail: info@maura
    daniel.com
www.mauradaniel.com

MAYA ROMANOFF
Phone: 773-465-6909
www.mayaromanoff.com

MICHAEL LEVINE INC.
www.mlfabric.com

MICHELLE LONG,
STYLIST AND WEB
BOUTIQUE OWNER
www.boholuxe.com

O | OBSOLETE
222 Main Street
Venice, CA 90291
Phone: 310-399-0024
Fax: 310-399-2155
E-mail: inquiries
    @obsoleteinc.com
www.obsoleteinc.com

P | PATIO CULTURE
1612 Abbot Kinney Boulevard
Venice, CA 90291
Phone: 310-314-9700
Fax: 310-314-9710
E-mail: info@patio
    culture.com
www.patioculture.com

PINDLER AND PINDLER
INC.
Phone: 805-531-9090
www.pindler.com

PLANTATION
1340 Abbot Kinney Boulevard
Venice, CA 90291
Phone: 310-392-6888
Fax: 310-392-6270
www.plantationla.com

POLLACK
Phone: 212-627-7766
www.pollackassociates.com

PRATT AND LAMBERT
PAINTS
Phone: 800-289-7728
www.prattandlambert.com.

Q | QUADRILLE FABRICS,
CHINA SEAS
Phone: 201-792-5959
www.quadrillefabrics.com

R | ROMANTIC HOMES
MAGAZINE
Phone: 714-939-9991
www.romantichomes.com

ROSE BOWL FLEA
MARKET
Pasadena, CA
Phone: 323-560-7469
www.rgcshows.com

S | S. HARRIS
Phone: 800-999-5600
www.sharris.com

SANTA MONICA AIRPORT
OUTDOOR ANTIQUE &
COLLECTIBLE MARKET
Santa Monica, CA
Phone: 323-933-2511
www.santamonicaairport
antiquemarket.com

SCALAMANDRÉ
Phone: 631-467-8800
www.scalamandre.com

SILK TRADING CO.
Phone: 888-SILK-302
www.silktrading.com

STUDIO COLLABORATIVE
Jane Hallworth
Phone: 310-854-0109

SWEETPEAS AND
SNAPSHOTS
www.sweetpeasand
    snapshots.com

SYNDECRETE
www.syndecrete.com

T | TARGET
Phone: 800-591-3869
www.target.com

TATUM CONSTRUCTION
Phone: 310-453-6666
www.tatumconstruction.com

TURQUOISE
1641 Abbot Kinney Boulevard
Venice, CA 90291
Phone: 310-578-1722
E-mail: turquoise.la
    @gmail.com
www.turquoise-la.com

U | URBANGARDENS
TEXTILES, SUSAN A.
REIMAN
E-mail: urbangardens
    @aol.com
www.urbangardens
    textiles.com

W | WALNUT WALLPAPER
7424 Beverly Boulevard
Los Angeles, CA 90036
Phone: 323-932-9166
www.walnutwallpaper.com

WEEGO HOME
2939 Main Street
Santa Monica, CA 90405
Phone: 1-800-65weego
www.weegohome.com

WERTZ BROTHERS
ANTIQUE MART
1607 Lincoln Boulevard
Santa Monica, CA
Phone: 310-452-1800
www.wertzbrothers.com

WILLIAMS STUDIO
David Jordan Williams
    Design + Photography
Phone: 310-204-1941
www.williamsstudio.com

# fashion resources

**A** | AKIKO OGAWA
www.a-primary.com

ALANNAH HILL
Phone: 61-3-9429-0000
www.alannahhill.com.au

ALEXANDER MCQUEEN
Phone: 323-782-4938
www.alexandermcqueen.com

ALICE ROI
Phone: 212-219-3305
www.aliceroi.com

AMAYA ARZUAGA
Phone: 44-207-935-9393
www.amayaarzuaga.com

ANNA MOLINARI
Phone: 059-637511
www.annamolinari.it

ANNA SUI
Phone: 212-768-1004
www.annasui.com

ANTONIO BERARDI
Phone: 39-02-87388749
www.antonioberardi.com

ARMANI
Phone: 212-988-9191
www.giorgioarmani.com

**B** | BADGLEY MISCHKA
Phone: 310-248-3750
www.badgleymischka.com

BALENCIAGA
Phone: 212-279-4440
www.balenciaga.com

BEHNAZ SARAFPOUR
Phone: 212-242-2343
www.behnazsarafpour.com

BETSEY JOHNSON
Phone: 800-407-6001
www.betseyjohnson.com

BILL BLASS
Phone: 212-221-6660
www.billblass.com

BLUGIRL
Phone: 059-637511
www.annamolinari.it

BURBERRY
Phone: 866-589-0499
www.burberry.com

**C** | CACHAREL
Phone: 212-410-9039
www.cacharel.com

CALVIN KLEIN
Phone: 865-513-0513
www.calvinklein.com

CARMEN MARC VALVO
Phone: 888-4-CARMEN
www.carmenmarcvalvo.com

CAROLINA HERRERA
Phone: 212-249-6552
www.carolinaherrera.com

CHANEL
Phone: 800-550-0005
www.chanel.com

CHLOÉ
Phone: 212-957-1100
www.chloe.com

CHRISTIAN AUDIGIER
Phone: 310-945-3232
www.donedhardy.com

CHRISTIAN DIOR
Phone: 310-659-5875
www.diorcouture.com

CHRISTIAN LACROIX
Phone: 212-753-2575
www.christian-lacroix.fr

COURRÈGES
Phone: 01-53-67-3000
www.courreges.com

CUSTO BARCELONA
Phone: 310-360-8088
www.custo-barcelona.com

CYNTHIA ROWLEY
Phone: 212-242-0847
www.cynthiarowley.com

**D** | D SQUARED
Phone: 39-02-8969-1699
www.dsquared2.com

DIANE VON
FURSTENBERG
Phone: 888-472-2383
www.dvf.com

DONNA KARAN
Phone: 800-231-0884
www.donnakaran.com

**E** | EDUN
Phone: 212-274-1521
www.edunonline.com

ELIE SAAB
Phone: 44-2-207-173-6424
www.eliesaab.com

EMANUEL UNGARO
Phone: 33-0-153-57-0000
www.ungaro.com

EMILIO PUCCI
Phone: 714-641-5669
www.emiliopucci.com

ETRO
Phone: 212-247-1200
www.etro.com

F | FLORENCE BROADHURST
Phone: 61-2-8338-8400
www.signatureprints.com.au

FRANCK SORBIER
Phone: 01-43-38-02-14
www.francksorbier.com

G | GAS
Phone: 39-0445-894000
www.gasjeans.com

GUCCI
Phone: 877-482-2430
www.gucci.com

H | HERMÈS
Phone: 800-441-4488
www.hermes.com

I | ISSEY MIYAKE
Phone: 212-226-0100
www.isseymiyake.co.jp

J | JUICY COUTURE
Phone: 310-317-9240
www.juicycouture.com

K | KENZO
Phone: 866-536-9687
www.kenzousa.com

KRIZIA
Phone: 0-26-20261
www.krizia.net

L | LACOSTE
Phone: 310-289-7700
www.lacoste.com

LANCETTI
E-mail: info@lancetti.com
www.lancetti.com

LELA ROSE
Phone: 212-947-9204
www.lelarose.com

LEONARD
Phone: 01-42-65-5353
www.leonardparis.com

LILLY PULITZER
Phone: 631-907-9112
www.lillypulitzer.com

LINDA LOUDERMILK
Phone: 323-233-8111
www.lindaloudermilk.com

LOOMSTATE
Phone: 212-219-2300
www.loomstate.org

LUELLA BARTLEY
Phone: 44-0-20-7368-8880
www.luella.com

M | MARIMEKKO
Phone: 358-9-758-71
www.marimekkostory.com

MARNI
Phone: 212-343-3912
www.marni.com

MARTIN MARGIELA
Phone: 646-613-8457
www.martinmargiela.com

MATTHEW WILLIAMSON
Phone: 44-20-7491-6220
www.matthewwilliamson.
    com

MENICHETTI
Phone: 39-02-5412-2091
www.menichetti.com

MICHAEL KORS
Phone: 800-908-1157
www.michaelkors.com

MISSONI
Phone: 212-517-9339
www.missoni.com

MIU MIU
Phone: 310-247-2227
www.miumiu.com

MONIQUE LHUILLIER
Phone: 213-747-8811
www.moniquelhuillier.com

MOSCHINO
Phone: 39-02-6787731
www.moschino.it

N | NICOLE MILLER
Phone: 888-300-6258
www.nicolemiller.com

O | OSCAR DE LA RENTA
Phone: 323-653-0220
www.oscardelarenta.com

P | PACO RABANNE
Phone: 33-155-9053-55
www.pacorabanne.com

PAUL HARNDEN
www.paulharnden
    shoemakers.co

PAUL SMITH
Phone: 44-115-9685979
www.paulsmith.co.uk

PERRY ELLIS
Phone: 800-994-0073
www.perryellis.com

PHILIP TREACY
Phone: 44-207-738-8080
www.philiptreacy.co.uk

PIERRE CARDIN
www.pierrecardin.com

PRADA
Phone: 310-278-8661
www.prada.com

R | RALPH LAUREN
Phone: 888-475-7674
www.ralphlauren.com

REBECCA TAYLOR
Phone: 212-967-0801
www.rebeccataylor.com

ROBERTO CAVALLI
Phone: 310-276-6006
www.robertocavalli.com

RODARTE
Phone: 213-221-4018
www.rodarte.net

ROGER VIVIER
Phone: 212-861-5371
www.rogervivier.com

S | STELLA MCCARTNEY
Phone: 310-273-7051
www.stellamccartney.com

SUSAN CIANCIOLO
www.susancianciolo.com

T | TOCCA
Phone: 866-325-7122
www.tocca.com

TOMMY HILFIGER
Phone: 646-638-4812
www.tommy.com

TORY BURCH
Phone: 866-480-8679
www.toryburch.com

TSURMORI CHISATO
www.tsumorichisato.com

V | VIVIENNE WESTWOOD
Phone: 44-20-7924-4747
www.viviennewestwood.com

Y | YVES SAINT LAURENT
Phone: 310-271-4110
www.ysl.com

Z | ZAC POSEN
www.zacposen.com

# acknowledgments

THE PROCESS OF CREATING THIS BOOK WOULD not have been the amazing journey it has turned out to be without the following people:

My husband, Clay, thank you for supporting my creative spirit. Your support has made it possible for so many of my dreams to come true.

My children, Olivia, Ella, Lena, and Joe, who teach me every day about life's possibilities. Thank you for helping me maintain my balance.

Suzie Domnick, thank you for always having faith in my vision.

Judy Pray, Rosy Ngo, Jane Treuhaft, and Doris Cooper, who helped guide and nurture this project over and over again. Jan Derevjanik, Patricia Shaw, Kim Tyner, Donna Passannante, and Ava Kavyani, thank you all for working your creative mastery on this book.

Karyn Millet, whose dedication and patience throughout this project have been amazing. Your photos speak a thousand words.

Bret Gum, thank you for your humor and interest in everything. Your curious mind is a great thing.

The manuscript people, Laura Murphy, Jennifer Gibbs, Barbara Jacksier, and Leslie Billera. Thank you for your outlines, suggestions, and words of wisdom. Darra Baker, you saved the day! I am ever so grateful.

Hannah Bagge, who made all things happen. I could not have done this project without you. Your organization, research, and dedication helped make this book possible.

The original road warriors, Alexandra Tumbras, Jennifer Hogabaom, Stephanie Coury, and Cynthia Brown. Thank you for helping me process my thoughts and ideas into reality.

All the home owners who graciously opened their doors to our crew. Thank you for your generosity and hospitality. You are the inspiration for a happy home.

All the shop owners who generously lent and supplied product and ideas for this book. Thank you for helping us create fantastic spaces.

All the girls at House Collections and Little House Collections. Thank you for stepping out into the unknown and pushing our possibilities for our team. Your running of the ship made it possible for there to be time for all of this.

My mom and dad, who taught me how to work and persevere.

And to the universe, for teaching me that it is important to swim downstream.

# photography credits

ALEXANDRA MARIE PFEIFFER TUMBAS ©
LITTLE HOUSE COLLECTIONS, INC.
pages 20 (left), 21, 24 (bottom), 27 (left), 28, 36 (top center), 40–41, 44 (top right and center right), 49, 53 (far right), 56 (top right and middle right), 61 (bottom right), 65 (top left), 68 (top left and bottom), 72 (right), 76, 77 (top left and right), 81 (bottom left and right), 84 (top center), 87, 92 (top left), 103, 117, 148 (top left), 151, 157 (top right), 199, 205 (bottom), 207, 220 (bottom left), 223, 231, 236 (left), 239

DAN LECCA
page 81 (top left)

DAVID JORDAN WILLIAMS © LITTLE HOUSE
COLLECTIONS, INC.
page 12 (left)

© FASHIONSTOCK.COM
pages 6 (left), 12 (right), 16, 22 (left), 26 (right), 27 (right), 29 (left), 31, 32, 36 (top left and top right), 53 (center), 56 (left), 61 (left), 65 (bottom), 68 (top center and top right), 69, 72 (left), 73, 77 (bottom left), 84 (top right), 92 (right), 101 (bottom right), 102, 109 (bottom), 111, 114, 132 (bottom), 141 (top), 148 (right), 156 (top left), 164, 181 (top right), 188 (top left and middle left), 194 (left), 197 (bottom right), 204 (right), 213, 220 (center), 229 (center), 237 (left), 245

© FASHIONSYNDICATEPRESS.COM
page 44 (bottom left)

FOTOLIA.COM
page 21 (right), © Vladimir Mucibabic
page 44 (center left), © Margaret Quinn
pages 52, 191, © Ploum
page 53 (far left), © OlgaLIS
page 56 (bottom), © Pavel Rozhkov
page 61 (top right), © Wolfram Zummach
page 95, © gajatz

KARYN R. MILLET © LITTLE HOUSE
COLLECTIONS, INC.
pages 2–3, 6 (right), 7, 8, 9, 10, 13, 14–15, 17, 18–19, 22 (right), 23, 24 (top left and top right), 29 (right), 30, 33 (left), 34–35, 36 (bottom photos), 38–39, 42–43, 46–47, 48, 50–51, 54–55, 58–59, 62–63, 65 (top right), 66–67, 70–71, 74–75, 78–79, 82–83, 84 (top left and bottom photos), 86, 88–89, 90–91, 92 (bottom left), 93, 94, 96–97, 98–99, 100, 101 (left and top right), 104–105, 106–107, 108, 109 (top), 110, 112–113, 115, 116, 120–121, 127, 128–129, 134, 135, 136–137, 138–139, 140, 141 (bottom), 142, 143, 144–145, 146–147, 148 (bottom left), 149, 152–153, 158, 159, 160–161, 162–163, 165, 166, 167, 168–169, 170–171, 172, 173, 175, 176–177, 181 (bottom), 182, 183, 184–185, 186–187, 188 (top right and bottom right), 189, 192–193, 200–201, 206, 208–209, 210–211, 212, 214, 215, 216–217, 218–219, 220 (top left and far right), 221, 222, 224–225, 226–227, 228, 229 (left and right), 230, 232–233, 234–235, 236 (right), 237 (right)

© KARYN R. MILLET
pages 11, 26 (left), 33 (right), 64, 118, 119, 122–123, 124, 125, 126, 130–131, 132 (top), 133, 150, 154–155, 156 (bottom and top right), 157 (bottom), 174, 178–179, 180, 181 (top left), 190, 195, 196–197, 197 (top right), 198, 202, 203, 204 (left), 205 (top)

MELISSA SNYDER © LITTLE HOUSE
COLLECTIONS, INC.
pages 240–241

© PAUL COSTELLO
page 4

PAULETTE COLE (PROVIDED PHOTOS),
PHOTOGRAPHED BY SHEILA BROWN
pages 238, 242–243, 244

# index

31901050470006